FEMALE ADOLESCENCE

Katherine Dalsimer

FEMALE ADOLESCENCE

Psychoanalytic Reflections on Literature

Yale University Press
New Haven and London

Excerpts from *The Member of the Wedding* by Carson McCullers. Copyright 1946 by Carson McCullers. Copyright © renewed 1947 by Floria V. Lasky. Reprinted by permission of Houghton Mifflin Company and Hutchinson Publishing Group Limited.

Excerpts from *The Prime of Miss Jean Brodie* by Muriel Spark (J. B. Lippincott). Copyright © 1961 by Muriel Spark. Reprinted by permission of Harper & Row, Publishers, Inc. and Harold Ober Associates Incorporated.

Excerpts from *Anne Frank: The Diary of a Young Girl* by Anne Frank, copyright 1952 by Otto Frank. Reprinted by permission of Doubleday & Company, Inc. and Vallentine Mitchell & Co Ltd.

The chapters on *The Member of the Wedding* and *The Diary of Anne Frank* have appeared in somewhat different form in *The Psychoanalytic Study of the Child*.

Designed by Nancy Ovedovitz and set in Perpetua type by Brevis Press, Bethany, Connecticut. Printed in the United States of America by BookCrafters, Chelsea, Michigan.

Library of Congress Cataloging-in-Publication Data

Dalsimer, Katherine, 1944–
    Female adolescence.
    Bibliography: p.
    1. Adolescent girls in literature.   I. Title.
PN56.5.A35D35   1985   809′.93352055   85–26389
ISBN 0–300–03459–8 (cloth)
ISBN 0–300–04031–8 (pbk.)

The paper in this book meets the guidelines for permanence and durability of the Committee on Production Guidelines for Book Longevity of the Council on Library Resources.

10   9   8   7   6   5   4   3   2

For Bob and Emily,
and in memory of Elizabeth Kamen

CONTENTS

CHAPTER ONE

Introduction

My subject is the experience of the girl in becoming a woman. It is a subject about which a psychoanalytic perspective is invaluable: our understanding of the development of children and adolescents has been richly elaborated in recent decades. While earlier formulations about development were inferences, "reconstructions" accomplished in the analyses of adults, more recent formulations have evolved from the direct observation of children and adolescents—seen not only in the offices of analysts but in their natural environments of families, nurseries, and schools. The scope of observation has expanded in time as well, both further forward and further backward in the life of the individual. What has been learned, in this enlarged context, provides a framework of extraordinary depth and breadth.

Where the account is wanting, however, is in its delineation of what is specific to female development. The ways in which it is wanting have become, in recent years, the subject of impassioned discussion—the revival of a controversy that began even as Freud was setting forth his views. With this renewed interest, many traditional notions are being modified, discarded, superseded. A more articulated picture is emerging of the development of the young girl which is different, in crucial ways, from the classical account. But this revision, thus far, has pertained primarily to early childhood. Her adolescence is just beginning to be comparably reexamined under the force of new questions.[1] Theoretical formulations in the past have tended either to assimilate the experience of the girl to that of the boy, or alternatively, to cast its difference in terms that are stark and grim. Whether the adolescent girl looks backward to childhood or forward to womanhood, it is a bleak perspective that psychoanalytic theory, traditionally, has offered her in either direction.

1. Of particular interest is the recent work of Ticho (1976), Barglow and Schaefer (1979), Blos (1980), and Gilligan (1982).

For a more clear-eyed vision of the girl's experience I turn to works of literature. What I shall do in the chapters that follow is to examine works of literature about adolescent girls in the context of a psychoanalytic understanding of developmental processes. My intent is to use theory and literature in a complementary relation. Psychoanalytic theory can enrich the reading of a text by highlighting, with its insights, particular developments in the narrative. Literary texts, in turn, deepen our understanding of psychological processes. Both psychoanalysis and literature attend to actual situations of human life; both register a kind of truth only insofar as they do justice to living moments or phases in the experience of any individual. The force of great fiction or great drama lies not only in the power of its language, but in the power of its insight into particular situations, which language delivers and which the reader, with a shock of personal recognition, acknowledges to be just. Psychoanalysis, too, yields insights of great power, but, emphasizing the *common* patterns in human experience, it tends to remove them from the sharp particularity of the language of literature, and treats them instead in a scientific voice. Theoretical formulations often give little hint of the richness of observation in which they are rooted. Works of literature invite us to restore this connection.

My enterprise, then, is a psychoanalytic inquiry, one whose observations are drawn not primarily from the clinical situation but rather from literary texts. My purposes are three. The first is to make more accessible to those outside the profession what has been learned through psychoanalytic observation about development during adolescence. The second is to use works of literature to explore in fuller range the distinctiveness of the female experience. The third I offer more diffidently: I hope that these analyses may deepen the reader's experience and pleasure in returning to the works themselves.

For I have made a point of choosing for discussion works which most readers will have encountered before. They are Carson McCullers's *The Member of the Wedding*, Muriel Spark's *The Prime of Miss Jean Brodie*, the *Diary of Anne Frank*, Shakespeare's *Romeo and Juliet*, and Jane Austen's *Persuasion*. These constitute, at first glance, an incongruous group. My discussion encompasses four works of fiction and one that is not fiction— a diary. This particular diary, however, is no longer a private document but has entered the realm of shared experience as works of literature do. Fictional characters, unlike the writer of the diary, are not real people. They are creations of language. But they live in the imagination *as if they were* real people. The reader of the work of fiction willingly suspends disbelief, in part, because the experiences of characters bear a relation to the reader's own observations and experiences, real or imagined. This resonance, I believe, is essential if the text is to have the power to engage, to move—to haunt the reader.

The Member of the Wedding is set in a remote southern backwoods town; *The Prime of Miss Jean Brodie,* in a private school for girls in Edinburgh. Anne Frank's *Diary* describes life in hidden quarters in Amsterdam during the Second World War. The setting of *Romeo and Juliet* is Renaissance Verona, and that of *Persuasion* is England at the close of the Napoleonic Wars. The texts vary not only in setting but in tone, in period, in genre, and not least in the gender of the authors. What these diverse works share, however, is that all bear in important ways upon the transition from childhood to womanhood, and each has the power to illuminate some aspect of this transition.

The order in which I have listed the texts here—it is the order in which I shall discuss them—obviously violates the chronology of their composition. It follows, rather, that of the age of the heroine, beginning with the twelve-year-old Frankie in *The Member of the Wedding*: for what interests me is the developmental progression from the beginning to the ending of adolescence. Miss Brodie's pupils are ten when they first encounter their formidable teacher and fifteen when they begin to go their separate ways; my discussion will concern the time, around age thirteen, when they are most intensely involved with her and with one another. Anne Frank was given her diary as a thirteenth birthday present. She wrote her first entry on that day, and she was fifteen when she wrote the last. Juliet Capulet is just shy of fourteen. Anne Elliot, the heroine of *Persuasion,* is twenty-seven, but she is absorbed in looking back to a decision she made when she was nineteen. What I wish to consider in this context is the difference between nineteen and twenty-seven—that is, the resolution of adolescence.

In selecting texts, I have deliberately avoided those which reflect a knowledge, on the writer's part, of psychoanalytic theory: two of the works, indeed, were written before Freud was born. My discussion assumes, simply, that a work of literature that continues to be read—for other than historical or scholarly interest—must resonate with enduring features of psychological reality, and that this resonance contributes to the power of the work over the imagination of the reader.

The shepherd in *The Winter's Tale* laments:

> I would there were no age between ten and three-and-twenty, or
> that youth would sleep out the rest; for there is nothing in the
> between but getting wenches with child, wronging the ancientry,
> stealing, fighting—[III.iii.59–63]

These words were written in 1611. Shakespeare's shepherd identifies the
period between the ages of ten and twenty-three as one of heightened
sexuality, intensified irritability and belligerence, of violating rules, and
of disrespect for the older generation. The modern audience laughs, taken
by surprise at the familiarity of what he describes—and the familiarity,
too, of his rueful tone. There are other features of contemporary adolescence which the shepherd could not have envisaged. Where social
class was immutable, where women had no economic alternative to
marriage, where sons entered the trade of their fathers, the "age between
ten and three-and-twenty" would of course be different than it would
be at a time of unprecedented mobility in these spheres. Part of what
we mean by "adolescence," now, refers to the psychological consequences
of having choices to make. The question of what are the psychological
differences over time—and what are the continuities—is one that, I
believe, we legitimately bring to works of literature.[2]

Before turning to these works, however, I wish to establish a psychological context for their discussion. I shall, therefore, first attempt to
summarize—in broad outline—the understanding that has evolved
through psychoanalytic observation of adolescence as a phase of life, so
that this sketch may serve as background for the closer consideration of
texts.

Adolescence occupies a unique place in psychoanalytic writing. There
is a tone of hopefulness, a suggestion of freedom from the relentless

---

2. When adolescence began to be recognized as a distinct phase of life is an issue
about which historians disagree. Aries (1962) and Demos and Demos (1969) argue
that the concept is a relatively recent one. Stone (1977), however, dismisses as "sheer
historical fantasy" the notion that adolescence was not recognized before the end of
the nineteenth century. He quotes from the autobiography of Thomas Wythorne, written in the late sixteenth century: "After the age of childhood (0–15) beginneth the
age named adolescency, which continueth until twenty and five. . . . In this age Cupid
and Venus were and would be very busy to trouble the quiet minds of young folk"
(p. 512). Other historians have identified features very much like what we mean by
"adolescence" in descriptions of youth abbeys in sixteenth-century France (Davis,
1971), of young apprentices in seventeenth-century London (Smith, 1973), and of
Puritan youth in eighteenth-century America (Hiner, 1975).

determinism of the past that is absent from the discussion of any other period of life. This is the time when the influences of earlier experience may be modified and even rectified: the awakenings of adolescence, and its reawakenings, permit new resolutions to old conflicts. The world expands, now, beyond the family into which one was born and did not choose. Adolescence is a period of widened possibilities and of experimentation with alternatives, before the individual narrows the range of what is possible by making those commitments which will define adulthood.

Often the period is a stormy one, but its very storminess has traditionally been regarded with respect. This attitude is clear in the following excerpt from a classic paper by Anna Freud:

> I take it that it is normal for an adolescent to behave for a considerable length of time in an inconsistent and unpredictable manner; to fight his impulses and to accept them; to ward them off successfully and to be overrun by them; to love his parents and to hate them; to revolt against them and to be dependent on them; . . . to be more idealistic, artistic, generous and unselfish than he will ever be again, but also the opposite: self-centered, egoistic, calculating. Such fluctuations between extreme opposites would be deemed highly abnormal at any other time of life. At this time they may signify no more than that an adult structure of personality takes a long time to emerge, that the ego of the individual in question does not cease to experiment and is in no hurry to close down on possibilities. [1958, pp. 275–76]

More recent discussions would widen the limits of "normality" to encompass, for some, a smoother transition (Offer, 1969; Offer and Sabshin, 1984).[3] Nonetheless, a period of turmoil during adolescence is not necessarily considered an indication of lasting psychological difficulties. It may simply reflect the magnitude of the changes, both internal and

3. Solnit (1983) considers the conflict between the point of view exemplified in this quotation, which draws on clinical observation, and that of researchers who find that a smooth transition is more typical of the adolescents they sample. He points out that what emerges in the clinical situation about the inner life of the individual—dreams, wishes, fears, fantasies, private worlds of meaning—would not be expected to be elicited by questionnaires, nonclinical interviews, or by the observation of surface behavior. Each method of inquiry has its specific advantages, which are linked inextricably with its limitations.

external, which converge at this time, and the momentousness of the developmental tasks to be achieved.

For both girl and boy, the processes of adolescence are set in motion by a biological event—the advent of puberty.[4] Giving the body its adult form, radically changing its size and contours, awakening new urges, both sexual and aggressive, the onset of puberty creates the essential dialectic of adolescence—new possibilities and new dangers. The sensual, diffuse longings of childhood now become more focused. Fantasies that press themselves upon the imagination are at once more exciting and more frightening than earlier wishes: with the maturation of the body, moreover, these fantasies are now capable of fulfillment. For the young adolescent, there is anxiety lest the new, more powerful urges invade and disrupt the relationships with those who have been most central in the emotional life of the child—the parents. With the onset of puberty, therefore, it becomes essential that the parents be relinquished as the primary objects of love. This constitutes one of the most painful, but also one of the most significant, psychological tasks of adolescence.

Those who, in the magical thinking of childhood, had been endowed with omniscience and omnipotence must now be reduced to human scale. The child's admiration is replaced by skepticism; pride, by embarrassment; and respect, oftentimes, by disparagement. The suddenness and intensity with which childhood feelings toward the parents may be reversed is a measure of how urgent is the need to create distance where once there had been closeness. This need underlies much of the behavior that gives offense to the older generation: the flouting of parental authority, and indeed of all authority—the "wronging the ancientry" lamented by the shepherd in *The Winter's Tale*.

The withdrawal from the parents, necessary though it may be, is still

4. It is often observed, in contemporary discussions, that it is much easier to specify when adolescence begins than when it ends. Apparently the problem is not new. A text which dates from 1556, *Le Grande Propriétaire de toutes choses,* distinguishes seven ages of man, corresponding to the number of the planets. After childhood and "pueritia" (literally, "boyhood") comes adolescence. Its hallmarks are what we would now describe as manifestations of puberty: it is the age when the person "grows to the size allotted to him by Nature" and "is big enough to beget children." This phase begins at fourteen—unequivocally—but defining its end point is more difficult. The sixteenth-century text grasps futilely at earlier authority: adolescence ends "according to Constantine in his biaticum in the twenty-first year, but according to Isidore it lasts till twenty-eight . . . and it can go on till thirty or thirty-five" (quoted in Aries, 1962, p. 21).

felt as a profound loss by the adolescent. It is not achieved without considerable sadness and pain, which have been likened to that of mourning (Root, 1957; A. Freud, 1958; Wolfenstein, 1966). The comparison is an evocative one, suggesting the intensity of the grief and the deep subjective sense of loss. Often the pleasures of childhood become tinged, in retrospect, with an idealizing aura. As in mourning, there is a yearning for the past and, ultimately, an acceptance of the irrevocability of its loss.

But the metaphoric mourning of adolescence has important differences from true mourning: under ordinary circumstances the presence of the parents allows the adolescent to titrate the loss in degrees that are tolerable. Two of the works of fiction I shall discuss, *The Member of the Wedding* and *Persuasion,* invite consideration of the effect upon adolescent development of the actual death of a parent. The simultaneous need of the adolescent both for disengagement and for continued sustenance from the parents is reflected in the repetitive cycles of emotional withdrawal and return. This cyclic pattern is reminiscent of that of the toddler, whose exhilaration with the new ability to explore the world independently may turn suddenly to fear and helplessness; at this point, the small child hurries back to the mother, to venture away again only after the reassurance of being comforted and "refueled" (Blos, 1967; Mahler, Pine and Bergman, 1975).

In this process, the adolescent experiences a loss not only of the parents as actual figures in the external world; the experience is one of inner loss as well. The child whose parents had seemed larger-than-life had derived some of his or her own self-esteem by sharing in their (attributed) grandeur. As the parents are brought down from their pedestals, the adolescent feels a corresponding diminution of self-worth. The inner loss that inheres in this process is conveyed in the subjective sense of emptiness and void so often described in the poetry of adolescents.

Indeed, poetry is written, journals kept, music composed by individuals who will never again in their lives be creative in these ways. That the subject of this creative output is so often "I"—my moods, my beliefs, my uncertainties—suggests its specific developmental purpose. As the childhood ties to parents are in the process of being relinquished, but new bonds have not yet been consolidated, there is a period of transition in which an enlarged self-preoccupation must substitute—temporarily and partially—for relations with others. Keeping a diary, the chronicle of one's inner life, is ideally suited to the concerns of this phase; I shall consider more fully the multiplicity of its psychological purposes in discussing that of Anne Frank.

During this transitional period, self-disparagement and grandiosity often coexist, or fluctuate rapidly, creating a strange, Alice-in-Wonderland sense of confusion and discontinuity. The tendency of adolescents to self-aggrandizement was clear to the Puritans: they identified "pride" as one of the two characteristic sins of youth (the other being "sensuality"). The eighteenth-century description of young persons as "apt to be conceited, and to magnify themselves, to be desirous of vain glory and ambitious of more honor and respect than they deserve"[5] has a familiar tone; it could easily be transposed to a contemporary description of adolescent narcissism. The propensity of young persons to "magnify themselves" ordinarily subsides in time, as the withdrawal into the self yields to the establishment of new ties outside the family.

With the loosening of the ties to the parents, there is a repeated search for new relationships.[6] At first, this search characteristically turns to one's own sex: in early adolescence, friendship assumes unprecedented importance. The intense, often erotically tinged relationships of this phase are altogether different from the relatively undifferentiated companionship of preadolescence. The friend is often idealized; for part of what the adolescent seeks is to replace what has been lost as the parents are diminished in his or her estimation. Now, it is in the relationship with the friend that the young adolescent feels enhanced, participating in the qualities possessed by (or attributed to) the other. The young adolescent girl's "crush" on an older woman is another form of idealized and eroticized attachment to one's own sex, which I shall discuss in relation to *The Prime of Miss Jean Brodie*.

In middle adolescence, the search for new relationships turns, most commonly, from one's own to the opposite sex. With the body sexually mature, the threatened reawakening of oedipal passions, both sexual and rivalrous, makes it the more imperative that the parents be relinquished

---

5. Joseph Sewell, quoted by Hiner, 1975, p. 261.

6. I have followed Blos's (1962) delineation of subphases within the overall movement of adolescence, which I find very useful in bringing order to the mass of observation about a period which is, of its nature, marked by confusion and contradiction. Of course the clarity of these subdivisions exists only in the abstract; in life, the subphases overlap and blend.

Indeed, Blos's writings (1962, 1967, 1979, 1980) are essential to a psychoanalytic understanding of development in adolescence.

as the primary objects of love. This definitive turning away is expressed metaphorically in the story of Romeo and Juliet. Falling in love with those who would estrange them from their families, Romeo and Juliet translate into action the psychological conflict that inheres in "first love." Under circumstances more prosaic than theirs, the development of relationships outside the family allows the individual to move, ultimately, from the family in which he or she was a child to a family in which he or she is a parent. It must be recognized, however, that significant numbers of individuals, both male and female, develop and maintain intimacies in homosexual relations. What determines the gender of the final object choice, and how the developmental goals of adolescence are achieved within the homosexual context are matters insufficiently understood at present. It is to be expected that changing social attitudes toward homosexuality will be reflected in increased theoretical and clinical attention to these issues.

My discussion thus far has concerned processes within the individual and within the family, and in that small circle encompassing the first significant relationships outside the family. The discussion of late adolescence, however, must appropriate different ground, for this phase brings the developing individual more definitively into relation with some wider segment of society. This is the period when decisions are crystallized which will define adulthood; the individual moves toward making commitments with respect to lifework, to sexual intimacy, to values that are expressed in ways of living. It is the time, in our culture, when "life lies before one with a variety of conflicting possibilities and choices" (Erikson, 1959, p. 92). Coming of age in Samoa, as Margaret Mead described it, meant simply beginning to be, as woman or man, what one had always known one would be. Coming of age in America, Erikson suggests, means—or promises to mean—*choosing* from an array of conflicting possibilities.[7] Blos (1962), addressing similar issues, sees the essential task of late adolescence as the delimitation of goals—again, from a multiplicity of possibilities. He emphasizes that in the choice of lifework there is a chance to integrate earlier psychological conflicts which have not been fully resolved: it is through this process that the individual

---

7. That there are many in America to whom life offers, in fact, little choice is explicit in Erikson's discussion, which is a description of adolescence in privileged segments of American society. Other analyses which emphasize particular historical circumstances as the context of late adolescence are those of Keniston (1968), Lifton (1970), and Liebert (1971).

comes to experience selected life tasks as "meaningful, self-evident, urgent, and gratifying" (p. 132). With the making of these choices, the
commitments of adulthood come into view and adolescence draws to a
close.

The nature of these possibilities—and of the choices required—has
of course been very different for women than for men. And while psychoanalytic discussions of the earlier subphases make explicit attempts
to encompass the experience of both sexes, the literature on late adolescence is less even-handed. The sense of choice that has made the
period such an interesting one in discussions of male development has
been all but absent from discussions of female development. This corresponds, to be sure, to the limitation of the possibilities offered to
women historically. But in these matters, description inevitably shades
into prescription: the endorsement of *the making of choices* as essential to
psychological well-being has been muted in relation to female late adolescence. The premise underlying this omission is perhaps most succinctly
conveyed in the subtitles of Helen Deutsch's classic two-volume work,
The Psychology of Women. Volume one is called "Girlhood," and volume
two, "Motherhood."

This work, which remains the most extended consideration specifically
of female development, appeared in 1944, but the assumption that life
moves inexorably from girlhood to motherhood underlies much that has
been written until recently about female adolescence. Contemporary
discussions are beginning to address a wider range of possibilities—and
their psychological implications.[8]

At every phase of adolescence, not only at its ending, but from its
beginning, it is necessary to consider how the distinctive nature of the
girl's experience may shape developmental processes. For both girl and
boy, I have said, adolescence is set in motion by a biological event, the
advent of puberty. But this is a different event for the girl than for the
boy—and its psychological ramifications different, I believe, in ways that
have not yet been fully articulated. What is the girl's sense of her body
at puberty? How does she experience its changing shape and contours,
the awakening of adult sexual feeling? What are the meanings, to the
young girl, of the onset of menstruation? These are questions whose
traditional answers have been colored by the dark view of female bodily

---

8. See the panel (1976) at the American Psychoanalytic Association meeting, and
the volume edited by Sugar (1979).

experience that is Freud's legacy. Even as Freud was setting forth his views, as I have noted, they became the subject of controversy within psychoanalysis. They have by now been criticized on many points, which I shall not reiterate here.[9] What I consider most fundamental—and what is most significant in relation to my concerns—is that Freud defined away the possibility of pleasure, delight, or pride on the part of the female in her own genitals *as they are,* and in her own femininity. In this context, menarche, the signal event of female puberty, has been most often described as if it were a fresh wound, which confirms yet again the sense of damage that has burdened the girl since her discovery, as a young child, of the difference between herself and boys.

But traditional views of the girl's early development are very much in process of change, and require a new look at her experience in adolescence. In this enlarged context, another important set of questions concerns the nature of the girl's relation with each of her parents, as childhood ties become modified in adolescence. Most often the girl, like the boy, begins life in what will become a profound, intense, complex relationship with her mother: unlike the boy, then, the girl's first love

9. There have been interesting facets to every phase of the debate within psychoanalysis, and the reader may wish to explore the issues further. Karen Horney (1924, 1926, 1932, 1933) took issue with Freud on a number of fundamental points, and Ernest Jones (1927, 1933, 1935) wrote in support of her dissent. The lively debate within psychoanalysis during the 1920s and 1930s then largely subsided, to be revived in response to contemporary feminist criticism. During the period of calm between the storms, however, Clara Thompson wrote a series of papers (1942, 1943, 1950) which were the first to consider the psychology of women in relation to their actual social and economic position. It is not the penis itself that women wish to have, she argued, but the power and privilege that men in our culture enjoy, of which the sexual organ is merely a symbol. In this tradition, Moulton (1970) differentiates a number of possible meanings that "penis envy" may have, expressive of themes in the girl's familial experience. It is clear, now, that Freud underestimated the importance of social attitudes and of learning in the feelings of girls about themselves, their bodies, and their mothers.

Schafer (1974) presents a lucid critique of Freud's views on several major issues. Other psychoanalysts have disputed Freud's formulations with respect to the girl's supposed repudiation of masturbation in childhood (Clower, 1975), her entry into the oedipal phase (Parens, Stern, and Kramer, 1976), the presumed absence of vaginal sensation before puberty (Greenacre, 1950; Kestenberg, 1956; Barnett, 1966), and the notion that clitoral sensitivity must be abandoned at puberty, a view that is now considered untenable (Clower, 1975). For an assessment of Freud's views on early female sexuality in the light of more recent observational research, see Kleeman (1976).

is for one of her own sex. What are the reverberations of this asymmetry in adolescence? How does it affect the "search for new objects" that characterizes early and middle adolescence? And how does it bear upon the choices she must make toward the close of adolescence, in defining her own womanhood?

Clearly, the subject of female development has been a vexing one for psychoanalysis from the beginning. Freud took up the topic and set it aside, returned to it, and in the end was dissatisfied with his formulations. He concluded his last extended discussion of the subject: "That is all I had to say to you about femininity. It is certainly incomplete and fragmentary and does not always sound friendly. . . . If you want to know more about femininity, enquire from your own experience of life, or turn to the poets. . . ."[10]

This is what I propose to do.

10. The sentence concludes, "or wait until science can give you deeper and more coherent information" (1933, p. 135).

CHAPTER TWO

Preadolescence: *The Member of the Wedding*

C arson McCullers's well-known novel, *The Member of the Wedding,* is an odd and haunting work. It is set on the outskirts of a small town in the South during the Second World War; all that is happening elsewhere in the world, however, only dimly impinges on the concerns of its three main characters. These are a twelve-year-old girl named Frankie Addams; Berenice Sadie Brown, the cook, a black woman with one bright blue glass eye and one sad, dark eye; and John Henry, Frankie's six-year-old cousin. Frankie's father, a peripheral figure in the novel, is abstracted and preoccupied, away most of the time at his jewelry store in town. Her mother is dead. Through the oppressive still heat of the summer, Frankie, Berenice, and John Henry have stayed in Frankie's kitchen, whose walls are covered with the "queer, crazy child drawings" of the young boy, saying the same things over and over to each other until their words seem to blur together and sound strange. This novel, set in a backwoods southern town and peopled by characters seemingly remote from common experience, lingers in the mind of the reader with sharp particularity as to its locale; its evocative power, nonetheless, suggests that its themes reach beyond this particularity. What I wish to explore here are those related to Frankie's age and her stage of development.

Adolescence has been called "the second individuation process" (Blos, 1967), comparable to that which takes place in early childhood. The comparison is a suggestive one. Over the first three years of life, the infant gradually emerges from a subjective state of feeling one with the mother to become an individuated, separately functioning young child.[1]

---

1. Margaret Mahler and her colleagues have described these developments in children from birth to the age of approximately three. The overall process by which the inner representation of "self" comes to be differentiated from that of "mother" is called "separation-individuation." (The word *mother,* in this context, should be under-

In the early years, the child becomes more independent of the mother's physical presence and ministrations as he or she develops a constant and reliable internal image of her. Later, in adolescence, the task is that of emotional disengagement from what are now *inner* mental representations and *inner* relationships, a process that frees the individual ultimately to develop new ties outside the family.

Particularly at the beginning of adolescence, there is a heightened experience of separation, as the radical changes of puberty create an estrangement from the familiarity of one's own body, and the stirring of new drives necessitates the renunciation of the parents as the primary objects of love. At the outset, the adolescent carries an "enormous burden of the unexpressed" in bewildering new bodily sensations and lone fantasies that he or she is loathe to reveal (Harley, 1971), which therefore intensify the sense of strangeness and isolation. Further, in the shifting alliances of this period, there may be abandonments by friends, real losses in themselves which also potentiate the feeling of loss in relation to parents. The renewed experience of separation and loss often arouses in the young adolescent regressive longings for that state of fusion which preceded the first process of individuation.

In "that green and crazy summer" when she is twelve, Frankie Addams feels that she "had become an unjoined person," that she was "a member of nothing in the world." The physical changes now beginning, the new estrangement from her father, the loss of friends who are already initiated into the mysteries of sex—all of these changes make her feel increasingly alone and frightened. When her older brother announces that he is to be married, Frankie conceives a fantasy to deny this loss and the cumulative sense of separateness. She will join her brother and his bride and go everywhere in the world with them, always. She will be a member of the wedding: "*They are the we of me.*" In the face of the renewed experience of loss, her fantasy is one which obliterates separation altogether; it yearns toward that earliest period of life when there is only "we" and not yet a separate "I." Only when the impossibility of this regressive solution becomes apparent does Frankie find an adaptive res-

---

stood to mean the actual mother or the person primarily responsible for the child's care.) For a detailed discussion of the vicissitudes of this process, and the subphases by which it is accomplished, see Mahler (1963) and Mahler, Pine, and Bergman (1975). For further considerations of the comparison between the two phases, see Schafer (1973) and Esman (1980).

olution. Ultimately, she is able to overcome the terrors of her new separateness by developing an intense friendship with another girl.

Thus Frankie moves from preadolescence to early adolescence, sustained by the achievement of a new kind of primary relationship, passionate friendship. The importance of this development is that it is not
only the personal solution for Frankie, responsive to the idiosyncracies
of her own history, and an artistic solution for Carson McCullers; it also
represents a central theme in the opening phases of female adolescence.
In the character of Frankie, in the movement of the narrative itself, are
reflected states of feeling and inner conflicts that are characteristic of
this transition—distilled, here, by the art of the novel.

II

We know Frankie's age precisely, for her age, and the changes that come
with it, are matters of concern to her.

> She stood before the mirror and she was afraid. It was the summer
> of fear, for Frankie, and there was one fear that could be figured
> in arithmetic at the table. This August she was twelve and five-
> sixths years old. She was five feet and three quarter inches tall,
> and she wore a number seven shoe. In the past year she had grown
> four inches, or at least that was what she judged. . . . Therefore,
> according to mathematics and unless she could somehow stop her-
> self, she would grow to be over nine feet tall. And what would be
> a lady who is over nine feet high? She would be a Freak. [p. 16]

Even now her own image, in the mirror that hangs above the kitchen
sink, appears to her distorted, and she quickly turns away from what
she sees there.

At the beginning of the novel, in her shorts and B.V.D. undervest,
Frankie is introduced as a tomboy. She dresses like a boy, she has had
her hair cut like a boy's, and she calls herself by a boy's name. To pass
the long August afternoons, she, Berenice, and John Henry muse about
how each would change the world. John Henry would have rains of
lemonade, and Berenice a world where there were no separate colored
people. But in Frankie's ideal world, "people could instantly change back
and forth from boys to girls, which ever way they felt like and wanted."
The fluidity with which she thinks of herself, at this point, either as
female or as male is suggested by her getting dressed up to go into town

either in a Spanish shawl or in a football suit—while her friend just as easily took the other costume. When the Chattahoochee Exposition comes to town, Frankie is drawn irresistibly to the Half-Man Half-Woman of its sideshow, "a morphodite and a miracle of science. This Freak was divided completely in half—the left side was a man and the right side a woman. The costume on the left was a leopard skin and on the right side a brassiere and a spangled skirt. Half the face was dark bearded and the other half bright glazed with paint. Both eyes were strange" (p. 17). Frankie is fascinated, but also afraid of the Half-Man Half-Woman, disturbed by the secret bond she feels with this creature, whose freakish split mirrors her own.

Frankie's assertions of boyishness are attempts to deny what the beginning processes of puberty are every day making more apparent: that she is becoming a woman. It is this that she turns away from when she sees her "warped and crooked" reflection in the mirror. The anxiety she feels about growing up is evident in her attempts to stop the forward movement of time by clinging to her six-year-old boy cousin and regressively taking refuge with him and Berenice in the nurturing locus of the kitchen. In the stillness of the August kitchen, the three say the same things to one another over and over: it is sameness and repetition that Frankie longs for, as change is being forced upon her.

We may ask why it is that becoming a woman is so frightening for Frankie. Of her mother, we are told only that she died "the very day she was born," as if it were too terrible to name the connection—that her mother died in childbirth. What might be the fantasies, conscious and unconscious, of a girl whose mother had died in childbirth? We have some suggestions in another literary text, a story imagined by a young woman of eighteen whose own mother had died of childbirth complications eight days after giving birth to her. The daughter grew up to be Mary Shelley, and her story is *Frankenstein*—a horror story about a monster that destroys its creator. Mary Shelley's description of the creation of the monster, on a dreary night in November, out of bones from charnel houses and parts stolen from the grave, makes clear the inextricable connection between death and birth. The scientist, Frankenstein, who gives life to the creature through a "series of disgusting circumstances" in a "workshop of filthy creation," immediately abandons him. The subsequent deeds of the monster become Frankenstein's justification for having fled from him, but in the monster's own telling of the events, the murders he commits are justifiable retribution against the creator who "spurned and deserted" him and sent him into the world to remain alone. The confusion in the popular mind about which is Frankenstein— the name of the scientist is often ascribed to the creature, who is in fact nameless—mirrors the ambiguity in the text about who is the victim and who the monster, the abandoning parent or the abandoned child.

Similar confusions beset Frankie. In being born, she had "killed" her mother. Her own growth, at the beginning of life, had been destructive. And now, at twelve, that growth is suddenly accelerating, propelling her, as her arithmetic confirms, toward some dreadful fate—that is, "unless she could somehow stop herself." But this she cannot do. As puberty begins to transform her own body into that of a woman, the unspeakable connection is nonetheless felt. The unconscious equation suggested by the history of her birth is that in becoming a woman she is approaching death. As puberty begins to create the capacity for womanly sexuality and procreation, Frankie is filled with dread of its mortal consequences.

The narrative reflects these unconscious equations. There is a sense of violence and abrupt loss in the description of the spring when Frankie is pubescent, conveyed by the startling choice of words:

> April that year came sudden and still, and the green of the trees was a wild bright green. The pale wisterias bloomed all over town, and silently the blossoms shattered. There was something about the green trees and the flowers of April that made Frankie sad. She did not know why she was sad, but because of this peculiar sadness, she began to realize that she ought to leave the town. [p. 19]

The blossoming of spring this year mirrors that of Frankie's own body. The "suddenness" of spring, its "wild bright green," suggests a bursting forth of something new and uncontrollable, as she feels within herself; the silent "shattering" of the blossoms the end she fears. The fantasies that are awakened make her feel that somehow she must flee.

In one direction, Frankie is terrified by what she is moving toward; in the other, she is saddened to lose the safety and familiar pleasures of the past. This is suggested metaphorically in her being unable, now that she has grown taller, to walk within the enclosure of the grape arbor, as she had done when she was younger:

> Other twelve-year-old people could still walk around inside, give shows, and have a good time. Even small grown ladies could walk underneath the arbor. And already Frankie was too big; this year

she had to hang around and peek from the edges like the grown people. She stared into the tangle of dark vines, and there was the smell of crushed scuppernongs and dust. Standing beside the arbor, with dark coming on, Frankie was afraid. She did not know what caused the fear, but she was afraid. [p. 7]

She does not know what causes her fear, just as she did not know what caused her sadness. We may surmise, though, that at dusk, as darkness comes on and the world of objects begins to disappear, Frankie has a heightened experience of separation and loss. Suddenly she asks John Henry to spend the night with her, projecting onto him her own fear and loneliness. "I am sick and tired of him," she explains to Berenice. "But it seemed to me he looked scared . . . Maybe I mean lonesome . . . I just thought I might as well invite him."

She herself is frightened. The growth that she cannot control becomes a metaphor, too, for the other uncontrollable processes of puberty. "She was in so much secret trouble" at this time: "Besides being too mean to live, she was a criminal. If the Law knew about her, she could be tried in the courthouse and locked up in the jail. Yet Frankie had not always been a criminal and a big no-good. Until April of that year, and all the years of her life before, she had been like other people" (p. 18).

That spring and summer, Frankie is "scared and haunted" by the town jail, and she dreads passing it. She feels that its inmates, like the freaks at the fair, recognize her as one of themselves: "It seemed to her that their eyes, like the long eyes of the Freaks at the fair, had called to her as though to say: We know you" (p. 102). Although the primal unconscious "crime" which makes her one of them is having been the cause of her mother's death, there are new "crimes," related to the changes now starting to take place in her body, about which she consciously ruminates and feels guilty. She has engaged in sexual play of some sort with Barney MacKean, which makes "a shrivelling sickness in her stomach" each time she thinks of it. "She hated Barney and wanted to kill him. Sometimes alone in the bed at night she planned to shoot him with the pistol or throw a knife between his eyes." The magnitude of her transgression is unclear to the reader, as it is to Frankie; not until the end of the book do we learn that all that actually happened was some "nasty talk behind the garage." She has stolen a three-way knife from a Sears Roebuck store; she has taken her father's gun from the drawer and fired it. These petty thefts, too, become magnified through her ruminations. "She *turned into* a robber": the impulses that now beset her, both sexual and aggressive, make her feel not only set apart from other people but estranged from her former self.

The ways in which the physical changes of puberty disrupt the accustomed body image are nowhere more powerfully expressed than in the following passage:

> It was the year when Frankie thought about the world. And she did not see it as a round school globe, with the countries neat and different-colored. She thought of the world as huge and cracked and loose and turning a thousand miles an hour. The geography book at school was out of date; the countries of the world had changed. [p. 19]

The globe is Frankie's body; the neat and different-colored geography book of latency no longer describes it. This book is indeed out of date, for the changes of puberty have begun to transform her body, and with it her sense of self.

Frankie's experience brings into focus the sense of solitude and loss—the renewed experience of separation—that the onset of puberty often brings. With the awakening of new impulses and fantasies, it becomes imperative that there be more distance between parent and child. The sense of loss that this engenders is suggested here by Frankie's father's suddenly telling her that she is now too big to sleep in his bed and will have to sleep upstairs and alone. From this time, "She began to have a grudge against her father and they looked at each other in a slant-eyed way. She did not like to stay at home" (p. 20).

Sex separates her from other girls, too—those a little older who are sexually more experienced and knowledgeable:

> There was in the neighborhood a clubhouse, and Frankie was not a member. The members of the club were girls who were thirteen and fourteen and even fifteen years old. They had parties with boys on Saturday night. Frankie knew all of the club members, and until this summer she had been like a younger member of their crowd, but now they had this club and she was not a member. . . .
>
> "The son-of-a-bitches," she said again. "And there was something else. They were talking nasty lies about married people. When I think of Aunt Pet and Uncle Eustace. And my own father! The

nasty lies! I don't know what kind of fool they take me for." [pp. 10–11]

The older girls' initiation into the mysteries of sex is a barrier excluding Frankie from membership; for her need still to deny the facts of sexuality, including the sexuality of her father, separates her from their circle. In addition, her best friend has moved away, another reflection of the shifting alliances of this age. In contrast, Berenice still has her friends, whose presence, when they come to call for her, intensifies Frankie's feeling of isolation. Even her cat takes off in search of sex and a ladyfriend: "It looks to me like everything has just walked off and left me."

The spring and summer when she is twelve have been for Frankie a season of losses, each resonating with the central event of her life, the death of her mother in childbirth. When her brother announces that he is to be married, her feeling of abandonment is complete. Although Jarvis has, in fact, been away in the army for the past two years in Alaska, his impending marriage becomes the focus for all the losses she has suffered. To Frankie, her brother and his bride have no specificity or individuality: in her mind's eye, her brother's face is "a brightness" and the bride "also was faceless." All that is clear is the feeling of being abandoned:

> Frankie closed her eyes, and, although she did not see them as a picture, she could feel them leaving her. She could feel the two of them together on the train, riding and riding away from her. They were them, and leaving her, and she was her, and sitting left all by herself there at the kitchen table. [p. 24]

She tries to deny the pain, busying herself in cutting at a splinter in her foot with a large butcher knife. Proud of having "the toughest feet in town," Frankie asserts with some bravado, "That would have hurt anybody else but me," but soon admits her vulnerability: "I feel just exactly like somebody has peeled all the skin off me."

Her attempts at denial fail. Through the cumulative losses associated with puberty, Frankie "had become an unjoined person." In preadolescence she does not yet have restitution for these losses, and she turns to fantasy. This has always been a solace to Frankie. In the alchemy of her imagination, her alley cat becomes a Persian; the moths at her windows, butterflies. To escape the anguish within she daydreams of being elsewhere. Landlocked in a backwoods town, she holds a seashell to her ear and listens to the ocean. In the oppressive heat of the Alabama summer, she daydreams of Alaska and Winter Hill, and watches in fascination the snow falling inside her treasured paperweight.

When the prospective marriage of her brother makes the sense of loss unbearable, Frankie takes refuge in an elaborate fantasy: she will join her brother and his bride and go everywhere in the world with them, always.

> They were them and in Winter Hill, together. . . . The long hundred miles did not make her sadder and make her feel more far away than the knowing that they were them and both together and she was only her and parted from them, by herself. And as she sickened with this feeling a thought and an explanation came to her, so that she knew and almost said aloud: *They are the we of me.* [p. 35]

"They are the we of me." The underlying wish is to assuage the terror of separateness by regression to an undifferentiated state before there is an "I." It is the wish that Frankie momentarily gratifies when, sitting on Berenice's lap, "She could feel Berenice's soft big ninnas against her back, and her soft wide stomach, her warm solid legs." Frankie slows her breathing in order to breathe in time with Berenice, so that "the two of them were close together as one body." The same longing is reflected in her wish to donate her blood to those fighting in the war. "She was not afraid of Germans or the bombs or Japanese. She was afraid because in the war they would not include her, and because the world seemed somehow separate from herself." As her blood mixes with that of the soldiers, she will become literally part of their bodies, and thus dissolve her separateness.

In her fantasy of joining her brother and the bride, they are bound together so that separation is impossible. "The world had never been so close to her" as when, in her mind's eye, she saw "the three of them—herself, her brother, and the bride—walking beneath a cold Alaskan sky, along the sea where green ice waves lay frozen and folded on the shore; they climbed a sunny glacier shot through with pale cold colors and a rope tied the three of them together, and friends from another glacier called in Alaskan their J A names" (p. 59). Frankie sees her brother and his bride not as a man and woman in a sexual relationship, but as undifferentiated from one another. When she conceives the fantasy of joining them, the three form not a triangle but a symbiotic unity. The rope that ties them forever to one another—like the umbilical cord that was Frankie's only connection to her mother—expresses her symbiotic yearning. In the logic of childhood, moreover, the three are fused through the magic of their J A names: the name of her brother is Jarvis and that of the bride Janice. Now Frankie adopts a fantasy name for herself that will bind her to them: "F. Jasmine."

The fantasied regression to a state of infantile oneness diminishes her terror at being separate and alone. Now, she is no longer frightened:

> For when the old question came to her—the who she was and what she would be in the world, and why she was standing there that minute—when the old question came to her, she did not feel hurt and unanswered. At last she knew just who she was and understood where she was going. She loved her brother and she was a member of the wedding. The three of them would go into the world and they would always be together. And finally, after the scared spring and the crazy summer, she was no more afraid. [p. 38]

The forward movement of adolescence has brought, so far, only separation and loss. Frankie finds solace in a reparative fantasy, the restitution of an infant's experience with the mothering one. In this fantasy of merging, all the inevitable separations of the "second individuation process" are denied.

The regressive fantasy, assuaging her anxiety, allows Frankie in some ways to move forward. She leaves the protectiveness of the kitchen, where she has remained all summer with Berenice and John Henry, and ventures into town. There, "the world no longer seemed separate from herself and all at once she felt included." She experiences "a new unnameable connection" with everyone she sees, a connection "impossible to explain in words." This connection eludes verbal expression, I am suggesting, precisely because it is rooted in the epoch of life prior to the development of language. Now, walking along the main street in town, Frankie feels "entitled as a queen," her power derived from the relationship to her idealized brother-and-his-bride, whose projected omnipotence she now shares. This idealization is reminiscent of the young child's view of the parents (or their surrogates), whose glorified images are essential to the child's own sense of well-being. Thus, "Under the fresh blue early sky the feeling as she walked along was one of newly risen lightness, power, entitlement."

After the fantasy crystallizes that she will be a member of the wedding, Frankie for the first time enters the Blue Moon café, "a place forbidden to children," where she initiates a flirtation with a young man. Like her brother, who has been in the army for the past two years, the young man she chooses is a soldier. On her side, it is yet another attempt at restitution for her loss. The soldier has his own agenda, however, and Frankie is made uneasy, and finally is panicked, by his sexual intentions.

She is, however, interested for the first time in listening to Berenice talk about love. At any time in the past, she would have covered her ears:

> The old Frankie had laughed at love, maintained it was a big fake, and did not believe in it. She never put any of it in her shows, and never went to love shows at the Palace. The old Frankie had always gone to the Saturday matinee, when the shows were crook shows, war shows, or cowboy shows. . . . The old Frankie had never admitted love. Yet here F. Jasmine was sitting at the table with her knees crossed, and now and then she patted her bare foot on the floor in an accustomed way, and nodded at what Berenice was saying. [p. 82]

There comes a point, however, when Frankie suddenly stops wanting to hear what Berenice has to say. Berenice, in speaking of love, speaks movingly about the death of her first husband, Ludie Freeman. Listening, Frankie notices immediately that he died "the very year and the very month I was born": she is quick to connect his death—like that of her mother—with her own birth. Berenice goes on to describe how she married each of her husbands—who turned out to be drunk, or crazy, or no good—because each reminded her in some way of her beloved Ludie. One had a thumb mashed like his, another his overcoat. The implication of Berenice's reminiscence is the finality of death, the impossibility—no matter how strong the wish—of reunion with one who has died. Frankie senses that what Berenice is saying has something to do with her plan about the wedding, and at this point she covers her ears to keep from hearing more.

The narrative itself reflects Frankie's unconscious fears: with the forward movement, however tentative, toward femininity and sexuality, death enters the story. It is at this point that Uncle Charles dies. Although he is only a peripheral figure, unrelated to Frankie, his dying stirs thoughts of the other deaths that have touched her life, and finally of the fearful possibility of her own death:

> "It makes me shiver, too, to think about how many dead people I already know. Seven in all," she said. "And now Uncle Charles."

F. Jasmine put her fingers in her ears and closed her eyes, but it was not death. She could feel the heat from the stove and smell the dinner. She could feel a rumble in her stomach and the beating of her heart. And the dead feel nothing, hear nothing, see nothing: only black.

"It would be terrible to be dead," she said, and in the wedding dress she began to walk around the room. [p. 77]

Frankie's musing about "how many dead people I already know"— significantly, in the present tense—implies that the dead are indeed presences in her inner world, where they continue to live on.

Her fantasy of joining with her undifferentiated brother-and-his-bride represents, in part, the "return of the lost parent" (Jacobson, 1965), a fantasy frequently observed in children whose parent has died. The irrevocability of the event is denied, and the child harbors the belief that somehow the parent is still alive and the insistent hope of a future reunion (Wolfenstein, 1966, 1969). When this hope is not fulfilled, there is bitter disappointment and rage, as there is after the wedding, when Frankie is left "wanting the whole world to die."

Until reality forces itself upon her, though, Frankie uses a reparative fantasy to assuage her anxiety. The difference between Frankie, in the first part of the novel, and F. Jasmine, as she calls herself in the second part, is that the latter is comforted by a fantasy which denies separation. She uses a "transitional fantasy" analogous to the early "transitional object" that allows the child to separate physically from mother so long as he or she keeps her symbolically present (Winnicott, 1953). So too, the fantasy allows Frankie for the first time that summer to leave the protectiveness of the kitchen and venture into town, still feeling a sense of "connection," her own word for expressing the overcoming of separation and loss.

Now she is no longer angry at her father, because she has replaced his loss with a fantasy. She is no longer envious of soldiers, nor of the girls of thirteen, fourteen, and fifteen. "In the old days that summer she would have waited in the hope that they might call her and tell her that she had been elected to the club. . . . But now she watched them quietly, without jealousy" (p. 79). She can give up the tomboyishness that she needed and can allow herself some movement toward femininity. The name she adopts for herself is that of a flower. She enjoys shopping for an organdy dress for the wedding, and wishes, now, that her crew cut were long yellow hair; she will bathe and scrub the brown crust off her elbows. The partial transition from tomboyishness to femininity is reflected in the way she appears before Berenice to show off the new dress she has chosen—her cropped head tied with a silver ribbon. The incompleteness, as yet, of this transition is echoed in the background music of the novel, a piano being tuned in the distance that repeatedly stops after the seventh note of the scale, without coming to a resolution.

The transition cannot be completed until Frankie gives up her regressive fantasy. She does not, of course, become a member of the wedding. Jarvis and Janice go off on their honeymoon, leaving Frankie behind, sobbing and enraged. Once reality forces itself upon her, and she must relinquish the fantasy of merging with them, she is left again with the pain of her separateness: "She was back to the fear of the summertime, the old feelings that the world was separate from herself—and the failed wedding had quickened the fear to terror" (p. 128).

To escape this, there is a brief revival of her fantasies of running away, again with both male and female possibilities. Either she will go to New York, dress as a boy, and join the Marines, or she will take a train to Hollywood and be a movie starlet. There is also a momentary thought of running off and marrying the soldier; but Frankie recoils from sex, frightened by three memories that converge—the silence in the hotel room with the soldier, the nasty talk behind the garage with Barney MacKean, and her glimpse, as a child, of boarders having sex ("Mr. Marlowe is having a fit!"). These memories, real and frightening in themselves, are also more conscious screens for the ultimate consequence of sexuality—death in childbirth. Sex is still too terrifying, yet, "There was only knowing that she must find somebody, anybody, that she could join with to go away. For now she admitted that she was too scared to go into the world alone" (p. 127).

The resolution is in finding a friend, which is the hallmark of the early adolescent phase.[2] Friendship allows a sense of "joined-ness" that

2. Blos, Deutsch, and Sullivan all ascribe critical psychological importance to the relationship with a close friend of one's own sex at this time. Blos (1962) discusses these relationships in the context of the disengagement from the parents. The early adolescent chooses as a friend someone with qualities he or she would like to have—or commonly, projects these onto the friend—and in the friendship possesses them by proxy. The friend, then, is heir to the child's earlier idealization of the parents, and the adolescent feels affirmed by the relationship. Deutsch (1944) describes the distinctive qualities of intense friendship between two girls and the psychological benefits of such a relationship in enduring the difficulties of early adolescence. Of particular

is neither a regression to a state of fusion, nor yet sexual, but which moves forward. In Frankie's friendship with Mary Littlejohn, there is mutual affirmation and a sharing both of the outer world and of their inner worlds. They read poetry together, each validating the other's ambitions—Mary's to be a great painter, and Frankie's a great poet, or else the foremost authority on radar. It is once again the season of the fair, but this year Frankie does not go to the Freak Pavilion; no longer feeling a secret bond with the freaks, she instead goes on rides with her friend. She relinquishes her rage at her brother, thinking Luxembourg, where he is living, a lovely name now that she plans to travel there with Mary. Their friendship enables Frankie to give up her regressive longings and to begin moving toward feminine sexuality: soon after they meet, she reaches menarche.

Through the relationship with her friend, Frankie grows away from Berenice, her mother-surrogate, and from John Henry, her young cousin, her old boyish self. At the end of the novel, John Henry has died, suggesting the relinquishing of her self-representation as a boy, and Berenice is leaving to get married, representing the development of Frankie's autonomy which renders Berenice no longer essential for survival. In the final scene of the novel, Frankie and her father are preparing to move. Now, at thirteen, accompanied by her friend Mary, Frankie is leaving the house where she spent her childhood, the kitchen where she took refuge with Berenice and John Henry from the terrifying sense of loss that accompanied all the changes of puberty. Frankie can now leave behind the tomboyishness that was a denial of her developing femininity, and the regressive fantasy of fusion, which was an attempt to ward off the terrors of separateness and loss. Only through the friendship with Mary does she finally call herself not by the boyish name "Frankie," nor by the fantasy name "F. Jasmine," but by her real name, Frances.

---

relevance for Frankie, Sullivan (1957) emphasizes that in the relationship with the "chum," distortions in the self-representation may be corrected through the experience of seeing oneself through the eyes of the other.

CHAPTER THREE

Early Adolescence: *The Prime of Miss Jean Brodie*

Nothing could be further from the poignancy of *The Member of the Wedding* than Muriel Spark's small masterpiece, *The Prime of Miss Jean Brodie*. Witty, elegant, polished, wry—it is a comic novel, and it is gloriously funny. It concerns a group of Edinburgh schoolgirls and their relation to a spinster schoolteacher, a charismatic and eccentric woman who, for a time, dominates their lives and fantasies. The novel is a virtuoso performance; its interest is heightened, moreover, by certain ambiguities which have partly to do with its central character, the formidable Miss Brodie, but more to do with the presence of the author in her work. Where, precisely, does she stand in relation to the characters of her creation? Like the author, one of the characters—the principal observer and commentator—becomes a convert to Roman Catholicism. As a nun, she remains most tormented and unreposeful. Muriel Spark is concerned, here, with the relations between Roman Catholicism and Calvinism, between excessive romanticism and fascism; these are the issues that have chiefly engaged critics.[1]

But *The Prime of Miss Jean Brodie* may also be read as a superb rendering of the central psychological issues of female development at a specific phase. It may seem an unlikely enterprise to attempt a psychoanalytic study of a work in which we are given virtually no information about the lives of any of the characters prior to the age of ten, and one in which, as I shall elaborate, the narrative technique seems calculated to interfere with our "identifying" with the characters in the usual sense. Nevertheless, the work does draw us in, and the world into which we are drawn is that of early adolescence. *The Prime of Miss Jean Brodie* allows us to observe the inner lives of girls, the nature of their friendships with

1. See especially Lodge's (1971) discussion of technical aspects of the novel in relation to its religious and philosophical concerns.

one another, and the character of their attachment to an older woman. It conveys, above all, the "sense of erotic wonder in life" that marks this period. The novel renders with subtlety the distinctive quality of girls' emergent sexuality—which is altogether different from that of boys. *The Prime of Miss Jean Brodie* is a masterful evocation of the specifically *female* experience.

The Member of the Wedding ended with Frankie's finding a girl friend, which brought to a close the tomboyishness and loneliness of preadolescence. The relation with the friend becomes central in the next phase, that of early adolescence, when the most significant bonds are with those of one's own sex. The opening paragraph of *The Prime of Miss Jean Brodie* sets the novel squarely in the early adolescent period. Outside the gates of the Marcia Blaine School for Girls, a small group of boys has stopped to talk—but they stand on the far side of their bicycles, establishing a protective fence of bicycle between the sexes. The boys, as they talk, lean on their handlebars, as if to make clear that at any moment they may be off. The girls band close together. The scene suggests immediately the unease, the mutual apprehension between the two sexes in this period—the boys poised and ready for flight, the girls huddled together, aware of their imminent departure. Indeed, at this moment Miss Brodie appears, the boys scatter, and we enter the all-female world of the novel.

The book is set in Edinburgh in the 1930s. It follows, from the age of ten, the small group of girls who have been selected by Miss Brodie to become, under her special tutelage, the "crème de la crème." Her own curriculum differs markedly from that of the Marcia Blaine School for Girls where she teaches, and it is necessary that she keep a long-division problem always written on the blackboard, in case of what she calls "intrusion." On autumn afternoons in the school garden, the girls keep history books propped up in their hands. "Meantime," Miss Brodie intones, leaning against an elm, "I will tell you about my last summer holiday in Egypt . . . I will tell you about the care of the skin, and of the hands . . . about the Frenchman I met on the train to Biarritz . . . and I must tell you about the Italian paintings I saw" (p. 18). Still with their history books at the ready, the girls listen to stories about Miss Brodie's dead lover Hugh, who "fell like an autumn leaf" on Flanders Field a week before Armistice. As a result of their idiosyncratic curriculum, the "Brodie set," as they were known,

were discovered to have heard of the Buchmanites and Mussolini,

the Italian Renaissance painters, the advantages to the skin of cleans-
ing cream and witchhazel over honest soap and water, and the word
'menarche'; the interior decoration of the London house of the
author of *Winnie the Pooh* had been described to them, as had the
love lives of Charlotte Brontë and of Miss Brodie herself. They were
aware of the existence of Einstein and the arguments of those who
considered the Bible to be untrue. They knew the rudiments of
astrology but not the date of the Battle of Flodden or the capital
of Finland. All of the Brodie set, save one, counted on its fingers,
as had Miss Brodie, with accurate results more or less. [p. 10]

Eccentric, extravagant in her passions, a true romantic, Miss Brodie
is full of vitality, in contrast with the dry-as-dust spinsters who otherwise
populate this novel. She points out the difference herself when indicating
to her students a poster that hangs in the office of Miss Mackay, the
school's headmistress, bearing the motto, "Safety First." Miss Brodie
instructs her girls that safety does *not* come first—that Goodness, Truth,
and Beauty come first. She tells her pupils that her educational methods,
in contrast to those of Miss Mackay, consist in a leading out of what is
within them (the true meaning of the word *education,* she says, derived
from the root *e,* from *ex,* "out," and *duco,* "I lead"). In fact, however,
she continually stuffs them full of her own notions. Egotistical, autocratic,
she teaches her opinions as if they were facts. " 'Who is the greatest
painter of the Italian Renaissance?' 'Leonardo da Vinci, Miss Brodie.'
'That is incorrect. It is Giotto, he is my favourite.' " Her inner world is
dominated by figures who are larger than life—Anna Pavlova, Cleopatra,
the late Helen of Troy—and she continually exhorts her girls to emulate
these figures, to walk with their heads up, up, up like Sybil Thorndike.
Miss Brodie is in her own way an appealing figure, but we are ultimately
appalled by the realization that her hero worship, her elitism, and her
conviction that certain individuals transcend ordinary morality make her
not only a romantic, but also a fascist.

Before examining the novel more closely in relation to psychological
issues, I wish to note that certain of the author's techniques tend to
keep us, as readers, from empathically identifying with the characters in
the usual sense. To begin, there is the author's own attitude to them.
She observes the events of their lives—even their deaths—with cool
detachment, which we as readers seem invited to share. Second, there
is only one of the girls, Sandy Stranger, whose inner life we are allowed

to know in depth. We learn something, too, of the inner life of Sandy's best friend, but the others are for the most part seen from the outside, each with one attribute to identify her, an epithet to distinguish her from the others. Jenny was the prettiest, Eunice was famous for her spritely gymnastics, Monica for mathematics which she could do in her brain, and for her anger. Rose was famous for sex. Sandy was famous for her vowel sounds (she was merely notorious for her small eyes), and Mary's fame rested on her being a silent lump whom everybody could blame. We learn almost nothing about the girls' families, nor of their histories before the story begins. Finally, the author's treatment of time disturbs our usual relation with fictional characters. She plays with time, skipping both forward and backward, flouting our ordinary expectations of narrative structure. Most unexpectedly, she "gives away" the suspense of the novel, telling us early on which of the girls it is who will betray Miss Brodie.

The book opens when the girls are sixteen, then quickly reverts to when they were ten and first fell under the spell of Miss Brodie. From this point, although the narrative generally moves forward, there continue to be jumps both backward and forward in time. Just as we are drawn into the present reality, there is a "flash forward" to some event in the future, or we are returned to the earlier past. The effect is jarring, and the movement disrupts the illusion of the novel. But the sudden shifts in time are singularly appropriate to a work about adolescents: at no other period of life are past and future both so insistently present. In adolescence, progressive development necessarily involves some regression to earlier phases, in order that the old resolutions may be reworked at a new, more adaptive and age-appropriate level.

To allow for the necessary disengagement from the parents, the child's idealization of them must yield to a more critical appraisal. But as the parents shrink to smaller proportions, so does the adolescent's sense of his or her own powers, and the young adolescent's inner experience often oscillates between a sense of superiority and one of emptiness.

Someone like Jean Brodie is perfectly suited to fill this inner void. By virtue of her serene narcissism and grandiosity, she offers herself as a larger-than-life figure to be loved and emulated. Not only are her views on aesthetic and intellectual matters absolute ("Art and religion first; then philosophy; lastly science. That is the order of the great subjects of life, that's their order of importance"), she holds opinions on the correct way to do everything. Rolling up the sleeves of one's blouse is uncivilized, opening windows more than six inches is vulgar. She abrogates for herself an authority which she invites her girls to share. By participating in her aura of grandeur—and that of Anna Pavlova, Cleopatra, et al.—the girls strengthen the uncertain sense of their own powers. Their need, at this point in their lives, is reciprocal to hers. At a time when the equilibrium of childhood has been shaken and the adolescent feels uncertain of herself, Miss Brodie reminds her girls repeatedly that they are the *"crème de la crème,"* all "heroines in the making."

"Give me a girl at an impressionable age," Miss Brodie asserts, "and she is mine for life." Her assertion is wishful, however, because in the normal course of development the need for a Jean Brodie diminishes. At the beginning of adolescence, however, as the ties to the parents are being loosened, there is a powerful need to replace what is being relinquished. For girls, this is the period when friendship becomes more intense than it has been earlier, and it is the time, too, of the "crush" on an older girl or woman. Deutsch (1944) offers rich clinical descriptions of such friendships. She emphasizes the faithfulness and exclusivity demanded of the friend, the complete partnership in common secrets, often with sexual content, which heightens the erotic aura surrounding these relationships. These secrets constitute a sort of experimentation in fantasy at a time when actual experimentation is still too frightening. Moreover, the sharing of fantasies with another of the same sex gives reassurance that the fascination and desire are normal. Boys may figure in these confidences, but they hardly have a flesh-and-blood reality. At this time, the girl is most intensely involved with other girls and women: her best friend, the clique of which she is a member or from which she is excluded, a woman teacher she loves or loathes, a celebrity.

The passionate involvement with females reflects the fact that the girl's psychic struggles continue to center on her powerful bond with her mother. There is a reawakening of feelings from the earliest period of life, when the very omnipotence which the mother appeared to have for the very young child made her not only the first and most important object of love, but also the object of rage—for the disappointments, frustrations, and losses that inhere in the growing autonomy of the child. Both sides of this intense ambivalence become reactivated in adolescence (Blos, 1980). In the face of new anxieties, appropriate to her new stage of development, the girl longs to return to the protective mother of her childhood. But this yearning is fraught with its own anxiety: the regression to an earlier stage threatens her with the danger of feeling reengulfed by mother, with a consequent loss of her sense of self. The girl seeks refuge from the archaic intensity of this bond in relationships with other females. These relationships—with friends, teachers, figures from literature and history—preserve aspects of the original bond, but in displaced, attenuated, and safer form.

The inner world of the young adolescent girl is peopled most vividly by other females, and the world of *Miss Jean Brodie* reflects this subjective reality. The book is set in a girls' school, in which not only are the students female but most of the faculty as well—the headmistress, Miss Mackay; the science teacher, Miss Lockhart, who announces to each new class in modulated tones that she could blow up the whole school with the jar of gunpowder she holds in her hands but would never dream of doing so; the gaunt Miss Gaunt; the Misses Alison and Ellen Kerr, living with the memory of their dead eldest sister; and Miss Brodie herself. There are only two men on the faculty, and they are not fully differentiated from one another; they have similar names and at first seem to look alike. They are one-armed Mr. Lloyd and short-legged Mr. Lowther. The school was founded by a woman, beneath whose portrait in the Great Hall lies an open Bible with the text underlined in red ink, "O where shall I find a virtuous woman, for her price is above rubies."

Males figure in this world only as outsiders. In the opening scene, the boys were poised on their bicycles outside the gates of the girls' school, ready to be off at any moment. In the closing scene, the female world has shifted to that of the convent to which Sandy had retired when she became a nun. Now, the bars are those of the visitors' grille, through which Sandy speaks with a young man who has come to interview her. Although years have passed, the book ends, as it began, in a world of women, where males are peripheral, merely visitors who remain outside its gates.

Men are present only at the boundaries of the novel in another sense, too, in the two world wars that frame its time span. In the First World War, Miss Brodie lost her lover, Hugh the Warrior, and was thereby freed to create and recreate him in fantasy. The approaching Second World War likewise offers material to be transformed by her imagination. After a vacation in Italy, she returns to Edinburgh bubbling with admiration for Mussolini. Later she will admire Franco and Hitler, and will send poor Joyce Emily, a girl new to the school and eager to be in the Brodie set, to her death in a train headed for Spain, where she was going to fight on the Loyalist side.

Miss Brodie herself remains an early adolescent girl for whom men are still largely relegated to the safety of the imagination. Indeed, this is an important aspect of the bond between her and her pupils. They share a need to keep men in the shadows of unreality. In an early scene, Miss Brodie asks Sandy to recite a poem—it will refresh them at the end of the day to hear her vowel sounds. The poem Miss Brodie chooses is Tennyson's "The Lady of Shalott." She will return to this poem, reciting it herself with eyes half closed and her head thrown back. Listening, Jenny sits enthralled, her lips parted, and Sandy weaves it into her daydreams. I wish to consider, then, the relation of this poem to the issues I have been discussing.

Until the stanza which Miss Brodie has Sandy recite, the Lady of Shalott has lived contentedly on an island in the river that flows to Camelot, the seat of King Arthur's court, obeying an injunction never to look directly at Camelot. Instead, she sees life only as it is reflected in a mirror.

> Sometimes a troop of damsels glad,
> An abbot on an ambling pad,
> Sometimes a curly shepherd-lad,
> Or long-haired page in crimson clad,
>   Goes by to towered Camelot;
> And sometimes through the mirror blue
> The knights come riding two and two;
> She hath no loyal knight and true,
>   The Lady of Shalott.

Alone on her island, with no knight bound to her, the Lady of Shalott has been content, weaving upon her magic web in gay colors the shadows of the world that appear in her mirror. Her contentment begins to be disturbed, however, when she sees there an image of sexuality between man and woman:

> Or when the moon was overhead,
> Came two young lovers lately wed;
> "I am half sick of shadows," said
>   The Lady of Shalott.

Her contentment is shattered completely when the bold Sir Lancelot enters the field. In several stanzas of description, he is surrounded by imagery of fire and light—"dazzling," "sparkling," "glittering," "shining," "flaming," "burning," "glowing." His magnificence, flashing into the crystal mirror, proves irresistible. It is at this point that Miss Brodie asks Sandy to recite:

> She left the web, she left the loom,
> She made three paces through the room,
> She saw the water lily bloom,
> She saw the helmet and the plume,
>   She looked down to Camelot.

To complete the stanza that Sandy has begun:

> Out flew the web and floated wide;
> The mirror cracked from side to side;
> "The curse is come upon me," cried
>   The Lady of Shalott.

By turning from her mirror and allowing herself instead to look directly at the dazzling figure of Sir Lancelot, the Lady of Shalott draws upon herself the mysterious curse, and dies.

For Miss Brodie and her young pupils, the poem resonates with the fear of leaving the world of fantasy for that of reality, and of abandoning a position of narcissistic self-sufficiency. It affirms the terror of yielding to heterosexual attraction—to the flaming, burning, glowing of Sir Lancelot. There is safety only so long as men remain shadows in a mirror.

Their fear of men as dangerous sexual beings is substantiated in the one episode in the book in which a man does thrust himself into their world. While Jenny is out walking alone, a man exposes himself to her. She runs home, where she is surrounded by solicitous relations who coax her to sip tea and who report the incident to the police. Later in the day a policewoman comes to question her. The event contains, of course, enough exciting possibilities to last out the entire school year. However, as Jenny and her best friend, Sandy, go over it—and over and over it— what most engages their attention is not the man himself and what he had exposed. That subject is quickly dismissed by their agreeing that he was a terrible beast. Rather, what captures their imagination is the policewoman. Sandy immediately deserts all the heroes of fiction about whom she had been daydreaming, and falls in love with the policewoman who had questioned Jenny.

In her mind's eye, Sandy pictures Sergeant Anne Grey, as she decides to call her, "looking very nice in her dark uniform and short-cropped curls blondely fringing her cap . . . Sergeant Anne pressed Sandy's hand in gratitude; and they looked into each other's eyes, their mutual understanding too deep for words" (pp. 101–02). Thus, as is characteristic of early adolescence, Sandy recoils from sexual interest in the man and his genitals and retreats instead into a sexually tinged relationship with a woman—a woman in a position that is usually occupied by men. Sergeant Anne is a policewoman at a time, it is emphasized, when there were few women on the Force. In Sandy's fantasies, she herself is Sergeant Anne's right-hand woman. Together, "they are dedicated to eliminate sex from Edinburgh and environs."

While Sandy may wish to eliminate sex from Edinburgh, she, and the other girls, are most eager that it flourish in ancient Greece, in King Arthur's Court—anywhere that remains safely in the realm of the imagination, so that they may allow themselves, at last, to look. Sandy and Jenny are intent upon returning to the museum where Jenny had seen a Greek god "standing up with nothing on." The girls immediately agree that it is essential to get a better look, that this constitutes "research"— their name for their continual attempts to find out more about sex. They realize, however, that they will not be permitted to go alone, and they decide to ask Miss Brodie to take them. Miss Brodie, they are certain, would not notice that he is naked: "She just wouldn't see its thingummyjig." Their conviction that she is "above all that" is particularly striking since much of their "research" consists of elaborate fantasies about her love life.

One of the marvellous achievements of *The Prime of Miss Jean Brodie* is its evocation of the quality of sexual interest in early adolescent girls. It is presented as an intensely sexual time. Later, sex becomes one of the things in life, but then, it is everything. Although the girls shut their eyes when sex stares them in the face, at the same time they see sexual meanings in everything else. The shuttles of the machines bobbing up and down in sewing class reduces them to fits of uncontrollable laughter. When Eunice seizes upon a line in the Bible, "The babe leapt in her womb," Sandy and Jenny accuse her of being "dirty" and threaten to tell on her. They chastise her for expressing the interest that dominates all of their lives.

The atmosphere of sexuality in the early adolescence of girls is quite different from that of boys, and what is distilled in this novel is the distinctly *female* experience. While the girls are preoccupied with sex, they are also deeply mystified about what it is. They know that somehow it is the force propelling the events that they imagine—vividly and elaborately—and yet they are continually asking themselves and each other *how the impulse feels.* Jenny passes along to her best friend the information that it all happens in a flash. "You do it on the spur of the moment," she tells Sandy; this she has gleaned by eavesdropping on conversations about an employee of her father who was found to be pregnant. Both girls are puzzled, however, by the question of whether the urge would not have passed by the time she got her clothes off. As Sandy daydreams about herself and the hero of *Kidnapped,* she returns again and again to the unanswerable questions:

> Supposing that passion struck upon them in the course of the evening and they were swept away into sexual intercourse? . . . Surely people have time to *think,* they have time to stop to think while they are taking their clothes off, and if they stop to think, how can they be swept away? . . .And if people take their clothes off in front of each other, thought Sandy, it is so rude, they are bound to be put off their passion for a moment. And if they are put off just for a single moment, *how* can they be swept away in the urge? If it all happens in a flash. . . . [pp. 55–56]

In their attempts to fathom "the urge" the girls eavesdrop on adult conversations, pore over newspaper accounts of sex crimes, consult large dictionaries. What they do not consult is their own experience. It is clear that the girls are beginning to feel stirrings of sexual desire, yet they cannot identify these feelings. Each avows her intention never to have sexual intercourse and to marry a pure person. They see sex everywhere, all around them—in Miss Brodie, in Mr. Lloyd whose wife just had a baby, and in the parts of the sewing machines that bob up and down—but they do not recognize sexuality in themselves.

The force that dominates the girls' lives is both irresistible and at the same time elusive. What is "the urge"? How long does it last? These questions, which girls at this point find unanswerable, would not even occur to boys to ask. How "the urge" manifests itself is not a mystery to boys. All their lives they have had the experience of erections, visible and tangible; the onset of puberty adds the experience of ejaculation. Whatever a boy's conflict over his sexual impulses, the impulses themselves are undeniable. "The urge" manifests itself in boys in ways that are peremptory and unmistakable.

Moreover, language itself validates their private experience. There is a rich vocabulary of slang available to describe boys' masturbation. In contrast, *not one* colloquial expression exists in English to describe that of girls. The disparity, I think, is astounding, and its implications far-reaching. The pubescent boy, beginning to masturbate, understands by the very existence of terms in which to speak about it—even to think about it—that he is not the only one doing it. The pubescent girl does not have the benefit of this reassurance. The virtual absence of a colloquial vocabulary means that there is no easy, joking way for the girl to learn that other girls do it, too. Simply, her secret is unspeakable.

And the language of psychoanalysis tends to echo this disparity. The very terms used to describe the onset of puberty—in both sexes—are metaphors rooted in the sexual experience of males. It is customary to speak of the "flood of impulses," the "maturational spurt," the "upsurge of drives." These metaphors fail to accommodate the adolescent girl's very different experience of her emergent sexuality.

The puzzlement of Sandy and Jenny about the nature of "the urge" reflects the fact that the new feelings stirring within the girl are difficult to localize and elusive in their origins.[2] In their "research" toward clarifying the mystery, Sandy and Jenny are indefatigably on the lookout for any scraps of information they can glean. They are, therefore, acutely aware of Miss Brodie's sexuality, and of her relations with the two male teachers in the school. From their observations they conclude, rightly, that Miss Brodie is in love with Mr. Lloyd, the art teacher. She "renounces" him, however, since he is a married man, and instead she undertakes an affair with Mr. Lowther, the singing master, who is a bachelor. The piecing together of this information is the achievement of many whispered conferences on the subject. Together, the girls collab-

---

2. Another masterful rendering, in literature, of the mysteriousness of the girl's experience is to be found in *Madame Bovary*. Flaubert's description of young Emma, at age thirteen, in the convent school to which her father brings her (her early adolescence, too, is set in an all-female world) makes clear the fusion of sexual longing with religious devotion:

> Among the white-faced women with their brass crucifixes dangling from their rosaries, she gently succumbed to the mystical languor induced by the perfumes of the altar, the coolness of the holy-water fonts, the gleaming of the candles. . . .
>
> When she went to confession she invented small sins in order to linger on her knees there in the darkness, her hands joined, her face at the grille, the priest whispering just above her. The metaphors constantly used in sermons— "betrothed," "spouse," "heavenly lover," "mystical marriage"—excited her in a thrilling new way. [p. 40]

orate on an imaginary correspondence between the lovers, which ends
with the following letter from Miss Brodie to the singing master:

My Own Delightful Gordon,

Your letter has moved me deeply as you may imagine. But alas,
I must ever decline to be Mrs. Lowther. My reasons are twofold. I
am dedicated to my girls as is Madame Pavlova, and there is another
in my life whose mutual love reaches out to me beyond the bounds
of Time and Space. He is Teddy Lloyd! Intimacy has never taken
place with him. He is married to another. One day in the art room
we melted into each other's arms and knew the truth. But I was
proud of giving myself to you when you came and took me in the
bracken on Arthur's Seat while the storm raged about us. If I am
in a certain condition I shall place the infant in the care of a worthy
shepherd and his wife, and we can discuss it calmly as platonic
acquaintances. I may permit misconduct to occur again from time
to time as an outlet because I am in my Prime. We can also have
many a breezy day in the fishing boat at sea. . . .

Allow me, in conclusion, to congratulate you warmly upon your
sexual intercourse, as well as your singing.

With fondest joy,
Jean Brodie
[pp. 107–08]

The letter is a wonderful pastiche, mixing the high tone of romantic
novels with circumlocutions used in newspaper accounts of sex crimes.
The girls picture "intimacy taking place" not on an ordinary bed, but
in a mythical setting. It is on the lofty lion's back of Arthur's Seat, with
only the sky for roof and bracken for a bed, that Gordon Lowther found
Miss Brodie:

"Took her," Jenny said when they had first talked it over.
"Took her—well, no. She gave herself to him."
"She gave herself to him," Jenny said, "although she would fain
have given herself to another." [p. 107]

Imagining the scene, the girls can allow themselves to look because it is
obscured by a romantic haze. They had begun to concoct the correspondence when they assumed the affair to be a fantasy. As they slowly
realize that what they are imagining is in fact true, they end the correspondence, burying it in a damp hole at the back of a cave by the sea.

The girls' intense curiosity about Miss Brodie's sex life stands in striking contrast to their seeming lack of interest in that of their mothers. When Jenny's mother has a baby, it evokes no comment; the girls do not even "speculate upon its origin." Instead, they are intently focused on Miss Brodie. No nuance of her demeanor with the male teachers escapes their notice.

In early adolescence, the emergent sexuality of the girl makes that of her parents at once undeniable and unthinkable. The awakening of her own impulses allows her now to "know," more fully than she could have known as a child, about the sexuality of her mother and father. At the same time, there is a fear that knowledge will spill over into exciting fantasy. The issues may be faced with less anxiety in relation to adults other than her parents. Again, the novel mirrors as external event this inner state. Mothers appear only once and momentarily, peeking in at the door as Sandy and Jenny are having tea. The two mothers are immediately dismissed by a "look of secret ferocity" which allows the girls to continue their collaboration on the love story of Miss Brodie and the warrior Hugh.

Sandy and Jenny whisper their speculations about whether Miss Brodie and Hugh ever had sexual intercourse. The girls tend to think not: their love was above all that. True, Miss Brodie had told them that she and Hugh clung to each other with passionate abandon on his last leave, but Sandy and Jenny doubt that this means they actually took their clothes off. This line of inquiry ends in Sandy's declaring emphatically that she would not like to have sexual intercourse. Jenny agrees that neither would she. Her intention is to marry a pure person.

The girls' relentless attention to the sex life of Miss Brodie, real and imagined, stands in striking contrast, as I have suggested, to their seeming lack of curiosity about that of their parents. But when they try to entertain the notion of Miss Brodie actually engaging in sex, the same flickering of knowledge and disbelief persists. Excitedly, Monica reports that she has seen Miss Brodie and Mr. Lloyd kissing in the art room. The others challenge her and demand details to substantiate the allegation—and make the picture more vivid. But, although her answers leave no doubt about the truth of her report, the girls remain preoccupied for some time thereafter with the question of whether Miss Brodie is actually capable of kissing and being kissed. Similarly, they can abandon themselves to the imaginary love correspondence between Miss Brodie and Mr. Lowther only so long as they think they are making it all up.

But as the conclusion becomes inescapable that Miss Brodie is *in fact* having an affair with him, the girls have difficulty believing what they know.

Thus, the girls' intense curiosity about the sexuality of adults finds its object in Miss Brodie.[3] And she is well suited to their need. She is, as she tells them repeatedly, in her prime—and Miss Brodie in her prime has more vitality about her than any of the other women in the girls' world. Looking back at the age of seventeen, the girls "had to admit, at last, and without doubt, that she was really an exciting woman as a woman. Her eyes flashed, her nose arched proudly, her hair was still brown, and coiled matriarchally at the nape of her neck" (p. 170).

But Miss Brodie also in critical ways remains an early adolescent girl, arrested in that phase of life through which the girls are now passing.

---

3. Similar issues are at the heart of Colette's classic *Claudine at School,* first published in 1900. Claudine is a spirited, impudent, mischievous girl of fifteen, growing up in a small town in France. The setting of her story, which is told in the first person, is adolescence itself: she and her schoolmates are living in a curious limbo, as one structure, the old school, is in process of being demolished, and the new is not yet fully completed. It becomes necessary that they take refuge, for a time, in the Infants' School before they can take possession of what will be their new home. During the transitional period, neither structure can adequately accommodate them, and there is disruption—but also unprecedented opportunity.

Their opportunity is for peering into the lives of their teachers—above all, into their sex lives. Claudine is forever eavesdropping and spying, "forgetting" articles of clothing in order to return to the classroom unexpectedly and surprise her teachers. As in *Miss Jean Brodie,* the intensity of her interest in her teachers is matched by her seeming lack of interest in her parents. Her mother is dismissed from the narrative in a single subordinate clause; her father puts in brief appearances from time to time, only to demonstrate his obliviousness to his daughter and his absorption in the scholarly study of slugs.

The story Claudine tells reflects no conscious interest in her parents but an indefatigable curiosity about parental figures—teachers, assistant teachers, the headmistress, a provincial minister—especially the women. The presence of the boys' dormitory nearby, its windows facing those of the girls, offers little distraction from this preoccupation. Claudine accepts the attentions of a young man with a mixture of amusement and contempt, but it is Aimée, her pretty young teacher, whom she lusts after. Aimée, however, is jealously guarded by her own lover, the headmistress, who is also having an affair with the District Superintendent of Schools (who, in turn, fondles and strokes Claudine whenever he can invent a pretext to do so). And so it continues. The narrative is dense with triangles, of all permutations, heterosexual and homosexual. No love—indeed no lust—is reciprocated. In the inner world of the adolescent girl represented here, no satisfaction, it seems, is possible. But it is clear where longing is directed.

This is an important aspect of her bond with her young pupils. Her self-preoccupation is that of an adolescent. Her immersion in fantasy is normally a transient characteristic of this phase. Jenny and Sandy finally bury their imaginary love correspondence, but Miss Brodie continues to inhabit the world of her imagination. She is full of crushes. She is passionate, but only in relation to fantasy figures. Rose Stanley's father, a rich and handsome widower, had taken an immediate interest in Miss Brodie, but she thought him carnal. The men she loves are the dead Hugh and one-armed Mr. Lloyd, who is married and has six children. As time goes on, the story of Hugh is newly embroidered with threads from Miss Brodie's present life. It pictures her affair with the music teacher as well as her longing for the art teacher, so that the three men become fused. The long-dead Hugh is now said to have taken her out, at times, in a small fishing boat. (The music teacher lives in a seaport village.) Sometimes Hugh would sing, while at other times he fell silent and would set up his easel and paint.

Miss Brodie renounces Mr. Lloyd and instead undertakes an affair with the bachelor Mr. Lowther, which she does in a spirit of duty, if not of martyrdom. Though she sleeps with Mr. Lowther, her relationship with him is passionless. She is maternal and controlling, dedicated to fattening him up. Obediently, Mr. Lowther works his way through all the food she sets before him, while Miss Brodie questions the girls, who are visiting her at his home, about her real love, Mr. Lloyd. Shorter than Miss Brodie, Mr. Lowther looks up at her shyly, hoping to read approval in her face. The house in which he lives is still pervaded by the presence of his mother, who has been dead for four years. The double bed he shares with Miss Brodie is the one in which he was born.

Miss Brodie's relationship with her girls, like the bond of early infancy, is one from which men are excluded. She promises them that were she to receive a proposal of marriage tomorrow from the Lord Lyon King-of-Arms, she would decline it, for she is dedicated to her girls in her prime. And she demands a corresponding faithfulness from them. Other interests which attenuate their tie to her become the object of her scorn. Indeed, as the girls enter mid-adolescence and develop other attachments—as they become distinct as individuals—their need for Miss Brodie does diminish. But earlier, while the bond with her was most intense, the boundaries were fluid between her and the girls, and among the girls themselves. This finds its visual representation in the group portrait Mr. Lloyd paints of the Brodie set, "wearing their panama hats each in a different way, each hat adorning, in a magical transfiguration, a different Jean Brodie under the forms of Rose, Sandy, Jenny, Mary, Monica, and Eunice" (p. 162).

The longing of the young adolescent to escape the sense of separateness was explored in relation to *The Member of the Wedding*. Here, too, this longing is expressed, along with the anxiety associated with it. As Miss Brodie leads the girls on a walk through historic Edinburgh, Sandy looks back and suddenly sees herself, and all the other girls, as "one body with Miss Brodie for the head." Her perception is frightening, and Sandy immediately tries to restore her sense of individuality. She has a sudden impulse to act kindly toward Mary, the girl scapegoated by Miss Brodie and the others. She finds, however, that to set herself apart is more frightening still, and she therefore checks her impulse,

> since by this action she would separate herself, and be lonely, and blameable in a more dreadful way than Mary who, although officially the faulty one, was at least inside Miss Brodie's category of heroines in the making. So, for good fellowship's sake, Sandy said to Mary, "I wouldn't be walking with *you* if Jenny was here." [p. 46]

She continues to nag at her until finally Mary starts to cry. At this point, Sandy retreats into fantasy, converting the unpleasantness with Mary into a quarrel between herself and an imaginary husband. Thus, she invokes a heterosexual situation as a refuge from the intensity of feelings in relation to one of her own sex. Above all, it is a refuge from the regressive yearning and the terror this arouses.

In the course of time, most of the "Brodie set" move on. As the girls enter mid-adolescence, most of them grow away from Miss Brodie and from one another. They now have boyfriends; they develop interests that set them apart from each other; they become individuals. Eunice has a boyfriend with whom she practices swimming and diving. Monica does honors work in mathematics. Jenny is always rehearsing for something in the school dramatic society, and Rose achieves a certain popularity with the boys standing alongside their bicycles outside the school gates. In contrast to the whisperings and shared secrets that characterized early adolescence, by the age of fifteen, "there was a lot they did not tell each other."

Of the Brodie set, only Sandy does not move on. Her primitive identification with Jean Brodie continues unresolved. At eighteen, she has an affair with Teddy Lloyd, both living out as her proxy Miss Brodie's wish and at the same time competing with her. Then, in a further, desperate attempt to separate from her, Sandy sets out to destroy Miss Brodie's career. It is she who betrays Miss Brodie, by giving the headmistress the information she needs finally to force her resignation. Neither of these acts, however, resolves the inner conflict, and Sandy remains trapped in ambivalent bondage to Jean Brodie. Sandy converts to Catholicism, adopting the faith of Mr. Lloyd though she discards the man; she is drawn to the Church of Rome that Miss Brodie disdained—and the church in which, we are told, she would have been most at home.

And so the novel ends, as it began, in a world of women. Sandy has become a nun. The closing scene of the book recalls the opening scene, when the boys were leaning against their bicycles, outside the gates of the girls' school. Now, in the convent, Sandy is speaking through the visitors' grille with a young man who has come to interview her. In contrast to the other nuns who, when they receive their rare visitors, sit well back in the darkness with folded hands, Sandy leans forward, clutching the bars of the grille. The visitor has been drawn by the acclaim Sandy has received for her treatise "The Transfiguration of the Commonplace." Its title bears the unmistakable imprint of her teacher. As in the opening scene, the young man remains outside the gates of the female world, and does not understand the richness or complexities of the world from which he is excluded. Naïvely, he is questioning Sandy about the major influences of her youth, whether they were literary or political or religious. Sandy replies simply, "There was a Miss Jean Brodie in her prime."

CHAPTER FOUR

Middle Adolescence: *The Diary of Anne Frank*

The *Diary of Anne Frank* is an astonishing document. It stands as a historical record—a chronicle of life lived under conditions of hardship and danger in a period whose events continue to haunt us. It is also the record of the inner life of a remarkable adolescent girl. Anne was given the diary for her thirteenth birthday, and she was fifteen when she wrote her last entry. The circumstances of its composition are well known. The Franks were Jews living in Holland who went into hiding to escape from the Nazis. With the help of Dutch friends, they and four other people lived for two years in hidden quarters above a warehouse in Amsterdam. It was three days after Anne wrote the last entry in her diary that their "secret annexe" was raided by the Gestapo and the occupants sent to concentration camps. Anne died in Bergen-Belsen two months before the liberation of Holland. She was not yet sixteen.

Her diary, which the Gestapo left, along with other papers, strewn about the floor of the secret annexe, exerts a powerful hold over our imagination. This comes in part from the effort, never fully achieved, to make sense of the period in which she lived, and to integrate its implications. But for the reader of the diary, the engagement above all is with Anne herself. Her diary reveals her to have been a delightful girl—bright, lively, curious, mischievous, whimsical, passionate. She took pleasure in the observation and description of character, so that her account of life in hiding glimmers, surprisingly, with humor. She was sensitive, too, to her inner experience, which she was able to articulate with delicacy and grace.

Anne Frank's diary records life in bizarre circumstances at a unique moment in history. Yet what is revealed surprises us not only by its extraordinariness, but also by its ordinariness. Even under these circumstances, we see unfolding the familiar processes of adolescent growth. Anne experiences the first stirrings of sexual desire and falls in love for the first time, confiding excitedly in her diary, "I believe, Kitty, that we may have a real great love here in the 'Secret Annexe.'" Through this relationship, she begins to disengage herself from the childhood bonds with each of her parents. She was able to achieve a psychological separation from them, even in circumstances which made physical separation virtually impossible. What we have in Anne Frank's diary, remarkably, is the record not simply of normal, but of healthy female development. Anne welcomed her approaching womanhood, took quiet pleasure in the beginning transformation of her body. She reflected upon her mother's life and imagined for herself a different future: increasingly, aware of her gifts, she thought of becoming a writer. We read the diary knowing that history would deny Anne that womanhood which she took pleasure—and consolation—in imagining.

Indeed, the very richness of Anne's diary may be due, in part, to the circumstances of its composition. Had she had a girlfriend with whom to share her secrets, she might have written less wholeheartedly in her diary. Had she had a circle of friends and teachers at school, some of the feelings toward her parents would have been displaced and attenuated. Perhaps the absence of a life outside sharpened her sensitivity to the inner life. How things might have been otherwise we can never know.

In this chapter I shall address, first, the wider context of Anne's diary—her response to the events of history and to the particular circumstances in which she lived. In the second section, I shall discuss Anne's psychological development over the period of the diary. At its start, she is at a transitional point in her development. Over the course of two years, we see the full emergence of conflicts that are characteristic of middle adolescence, and the beginning of their resolution. In the final section, I shall consider more generally the developmental significance of the diary itself—its relation to the specific needs of the adolescent period and to earlier acts of imagination of the child.

I

The Franks were an old German Jewish family. Both daughters, Anne and her sister Margot, three years older, were born in Frankfurt, where Otto Frank was a businessman. When Anne was four, the family emigrated to Holland to escape persecution by the Nazis. Settling in Amsterdam, Otto Frank succeeded in reestablishing himself in the food products business, becoming managing director of one company and a partner in an affiliate. Anne was nearly eleven when Germany invaded the Netherlands and anti-Jewish decrees began to follow one another in rapid succession.

All this is in the background, however, in the earliest pages of the diary, which begins several weeks before the family went into hiding. Our first glimpse of Anne is of a gregarious schoolgirl—affectionate to her parents, nervously awaiting the announcement of grades with her classmates, beginning to be aware that she is noticed by boys. These early entries radiate a sense of abundance in the love Anne feels from her parents and friends, a capacity for pleasure in other people and in her intellectual interests. She describes with delight the gifts she received for her thirteenth birthday: beside the diary itself, there were flowers, a party game, sweets, books. She is pleased to be given some money, so that now she can buy "*The Myths of Greece and Rome*—grand!"

Anne is a high-spirited girl with a mischievous streak—unlike her sister, Margot, whom she describes with a mixture of envy and condescension as "perfection itself." As punishment for talking in class, Anne was given an assignment of writing a composition entitled "A Chatterbox." Anyone, she observes, can scribble some nonsense in large letters with words well spaced; the task she set herself was to prove beyond a doubt the necessity of talking. Anne describes herself as having thought and thought, and then suddenly having an idea, filling her allotted three sides. Her argument was that talking is a feminine characteristic and she would do her best to keep it under control, but she would never be cured, for her mother talked as much as she, and what can one do about inherited qualities?

Anne's playfulness nearly allows us to forget what she, too, is trying to force into the background. In these initial entries, her schoolgirl concerns are oddly juxtaposed with the darkening shadow of anti-Jewish measures. She relates in a chatty tone that after playing ping-pong she and her friends enjoy going for an icecream—to one of the two shops in which Jews are allowed. In what was to be the last entry before the family went into hiding, Anne records her father's advice that she make the most of her "carefree young life" while she can. Later the same day the SS sent a deportation notice for her sister. That night, wearing as many layers of clothing as they could without attracting attention, the

Franks left their home and took refuge above Otto Frank's place of business in hidden quarters that he had been preparing against such a time. Here, they were soon joined by another family, the Van Daans, with their fifteen-year-old son Peter, and by an eighth person, Albert Dussel, a middle-aged dentist.

What immediately strikes the reader of her diary is Anne's courage and humor during the two years in hiding. As time goes on and food becomes scarce, she finds comical aspects to their communal efforts to scrape the mold from beans and to cut out the rotten parts of potatoes. In her chronicle of these activities, each participant reveals his character amusingly and memorably. After a year and a half in hiding, she even manages to be entertaining while describing the very monotony of their lives:

> What it all boils down to is this—that if one of the eight of us opens his mouth, the other seven can finish the story for him! We all know the point of every joke from the start, and the storyteller is alone in laughing at his witticisms. The various milkmen, grocers, and butchers of the two ex-housewives have already grown beards in our minds, so often have they been praised to the skies or pulled to pieces; it is impossible for anything in the conversation here to be fresh or new. [(14 yrs., 7 mos.)[1] pp. 130–31]

The earliest entries written in the secret annexe show Anne's determined effort to banish fear and depression by finding, somehow, a bright side. She compares their situation to "being on vacation in a very peculiar boardinghouse. You'd never find such a comfortable hiding place anywhere in Amsterdam, no, perhaps not even in the whole of Holland." The rest of the family cannot get used to the clock nearby which strikes every quarter hour, but "I can. I loved it from the start, and especially in the night it's like a faithful friend." Like the diary itself, her other faithful friend, Anne uses the striking of the clock to create an element of constancy in the face of overwhelming loss and dislocation.

She has only to look out the window to see what their fate would be outside:

> In the evening when it's dark, I often see rows of good, innocent people accompanied by crying children, walking on and on, in

1. In order to follow closely Anne's development, I have translated the date of each diary entry into her age at the time she wrote it, in years and months.

charge of a couple of these chaps, bullied and knocked about until they almost drop. No one is spared—old people, babies, expectant mothers, the sick—each and all join in the march of death. [(13 yrs., 5 mos.) p. 48]

In what she sees from the window, in what she hears over the wireless or from their Dutch friends, what takes hold of Anne's imagination is the separation of children from their parents. When she allows herself to think about the danger outside, this is the recurring theme:

Families are torn apart, the men, women, and children all being separated. Children coming home from school find that their parents have disappeared. Women return from shopping to find their homes shut up and their families gone. . . .

The children here run about in just a thin blouse and clogs; no coat, no hat, no stockings, and no one helps them. Their tummies are empty. . . . [(13 yrs., 7 mos.) p. 57]

And again: "You hear of children lost in the smouldering ruins, looking for their parents." Finally she allows herself to express the terror explicitly in relation to herself:

At night, when I'm in bed, I see myself alone in a dungeon, without Mummy and Daddy. Sometimes I wander by the roadside or our 'Secret Annexe' is on fire, or they come and take us away at night. . . .

I see the eight of us with our 'Secret Annexe' as if we were a little piece of blue heaven, surrounded by rain clouds. The round, clearly defined spot where we stand is still safe, but the clouds gather more closely about us and the circle which separates us from the approaching danger closes more and more tightly. [(14 yrs., 4 mos.) p. 103]

Conditions of daily life in the secret annexe became more arduous as time went on. Anne wore clothes she had long since outgrown, slept on a bed extended by a chair with a pillow, ate food of poor quality and meager quantity. But when she permits herself to acknowledge the privations of her situation, she feels guilty for complaining, knowing how much more fortunate she is than others. On the other hand, this good fortune is itself guilt-provoking: "I feel wicked sleeping in a warm bed, while my dearest friends have been knocked down or have fallen into a gutter somewhere out in the cold night" ([13 yrs., 5 mos.] p. 48).

Her guilt becomes focused on her school friend Lies, who appears before her one night as she is falling asleep: "I saw her in front of me, clothed in rags, her face thin and worn. Her eyes were very big and she looked so sadly and reproachfully at me that I could read in her eyes, 'Oh Anne, why have you deserted me? Help, oh, help me, rescue me from this hell!'" ([14 yrs., 5 mos.] p. 107). The rest of this entry is filled with self-reproach. In seizing upon some ostensible reason for her self-castigation, Anne reaches back in time and reverses the present situation, when she feels that she has abandoned Lies. Instead, she looks to their schooldays together, when Lies became attached to a new girlfriend and Anne felt herself abandoned. The content is unclear; whatever happened surely cannot match the magnitude of her self-accusations: "It was horrid of me to treat her as I did. . . . I was selfishly absorbed in my own pleasures and problems. . . . I can't help, or repair the wrong I have done." Anne's guilt is displaced from its true cause, which lies in the present: "Oh, God, that I should have all I could wish for and that she should be seized by such a terrible fate. I am not more virtuous than she; she, too, wanted to do what was right, why should I be chosen to live and she probably to die?" ([14 yrs., 5 mos.] p. 107). Anne's anguished questions express the guilt of the survivor.

Still, she could not help wishing for the normal pleasures of the teenager: "Cycling, dancing, whistling, looking out at the world, feeling young, to know that I'm free—that's what I long for." That Anne had such longings is hardly surprising. What is surprising is that even under conditions that made these ordinary pleasures impossible, Anne could experience the normal processes of adolescent growth and development. Through her diary, we may follow these processes, day by day.

II

The diaries of adolescents have been recognized as offering a unique mode of access to their inner lives (Bernfeld, 1927, 1931; Mack, 1980). In 1915, Freud wrote the following letter about the diary of a young girl that had been brought to his attention:

> The diary is a little gem. I really believe it has never before been possible to obtain such a clear and truthful view of the mental impulses that characterize the development of a girl in our social and cultural stratum during the years before puberty. We are shown

how her feelings grow up out of a childish egoism till they reach social maturity; . . . and, above all, how the secret of sexual life begins to dawn on her indistinctly and then takes complete possession of the child's mind; how, in the consciousness of her secret knowledge, she at first suffers hurt, but little by little overcomes it. All of this is so charmingly, so naturally, and so gravely expressed in these artless notes that they cannot fail to arouse the greatest interest in educators and psychologists. . . . [1919 (1915), p. 341]

Much the same might be said of Anne's diary. It complements our study of works of fiction in that, unlike these, the diary has not been revised or polished. It presents Anne's reflections, impressions, and feelings in spontaneous form, almost day by day, over the course of more than two years.[2]

I am suggesting that the richness of the diary for the study of development consists in its being not only the repository of secrets which the adolescent is otherwise loathe to reveal, but also a record of the flow of thought. We have an opportunity, analogous to that of the clinical situation, to attend not only to the *content* of what is expressed, but to its associative *sequence* as well. In the diary we can observe the order in which thoughts, feelings, and impulses emerge; we can look carefully at juxtapositions, associative links, omissions. We can turn back its pages, to study the context in which a new line of thought first appeared. We can note shifts—of subject, of tone, of mood, of style—which may signal points of anxiety. Attending to the structure of the diary as well as its manifest content allows us to examine the vicissitudes of conflict and its resolution over the course of time.

Anne's diary, as I noted earlier, was given to her for her thirteenth birthday. Her first description of herself, on the morning of her birthday, is of an excited child barely able to restrain her eagerness to open her presents: "I woke up at six o'clock and no wonder; it was my birthday. But of course I was not allowed to get up at that hour, so I had to control my curiosity. . . . Soon after seven I went to Mummy and Daddy and then to the sitting room to undo my presents. The first to greet me was *you,* possibly the nicest of all" (p. 1). The second entry, an account

---

2. This is not to suggest, of course, that the diary is free of censorship, conscious as well as unconscious. In fantasy, it is at once a private confession and a document intended for an unseen audience. In the third section of this chapter I shall consider the multiple, sometimes contradictory meanings of the diary to its author.

of her birthday party, reveals a charming mixture of childish and adolescent interests, which suggests that Anne is at a transitional point in her development:

> I had my birthday party on Sunday afternoon. We showed a film *The Lighthouse Keeper* with Rin Tin Tin, which my school friends thoroughly enjoyed. We had a lovely time. There were lots of girls and boys. Mummy always wants to know whom I'm going to marry. Little does she guess that it's Peter Wessell; one day I managed, without blushing or flickering an eyelid, to get that idea right out of her mind. [13 yrs., 0 mos., pp. 1–2]

Thus, when the diary begins Anne is still young enough to enjoy a movie about the adventures of a dog. The afternoon party, with its undifferentiated group of both sexes, is also typical of latency. The rapid shift of subjects, however, suggests the waning of latency interests and the earliest beginning of interest in the opposite sex. The latter is still relegated to the future, however, and expressed in the childish form of "Whom will I marry?"

It is noteworthy that Anne introduces her mother here in the context of keeping a secret from her. Her mother is always asking whom she will marry, and Anne has managed to deceive her. Why does Anne make a point of concealing her intentions from her mother? Peter Wessel, the young man she plans to marry, will return later in a dream, when Anne reveals more about him. He is tall, and older than Anne. They had spent one summer together, but he dropped her because he found her childish. Instead, he turned to girlfriends of his own age, of whom Anne was very jealous. The oedipal aura that surrounds this figure suggests why Anne may wish to keep her mother in the dark about her true intentions.

After mentioning the secret from her mother, Anne's thoughts turn next to her girlfriends. She goes on, with no transition, to write that the two girls who had been her best friends for many years have now turned away from her. One goes to another school, and the other, Lies, is now more friendly with someone else: Anne will later recall her own response to this with anguish. Her writing, here, of the loss of her closest girlfriends is not simply a literal recording of the fact. In the context of her associations, it becomes a metaphor for the estrangement that Anne is beginning to feel in relation to her mother. Although it is clear, and becomes more so, that Anne herself is withdrawing, her associations suggest that she feels abandoned, nonetheless. Here, in the opening pages of the diary, is the first allusion to a theme that will become increasingly important.

The sexual interest that boys take in Anne finds, as yet, no answering feeling within her. She describes herself as "taking little notice of their ardent looks" and "pedaling blithely on." If, in spite of this, boys persist in making advances, she lets them know that "they are definitely knocking at the wrong door. I get off my bicycle and refuse to go further in their company, or I pretend to be insulted and tell them in no uncertain terms to clear off." At thirteen, Anne's relations with girlfriends are most important, and boys remain, still, in the realm of fantasy.

Indeed, Anne creates of the diary itself a girlfriend. Each entry is a letter to an imaginary friend which begins "Dear Kitty," and is signed, "Yours, Anne." In the privacy of her imagination, "Kitty" comes to life as if she were a real friend who could be surprised, or saddened, or even bored by Anne's communications. I shall explore the meaning of this imagined "other" in the final section of this chapter; in the present context it is of interest that Anne consolidates their friendship by assuring Kitty that she is not interested in boys. After describing her techniques for rebuffing their advances, she concludes her letter to "Kitty": "There, the foundation of our friendship is laid, till tomorrow!"

Thus, the earliest entries suggest that as Anne begins the diary she is at a transitional point in her development. While there are vestiges, still, of latency interests, at thirteen Anne is an early adolescent who is beginning to experience the conflicts of the next phase. At the outset, the relationships that are most vivid emotionally are those with her own sex. Over the two years of the diary, we see this shift. What we shall observe is the development of the central unconscious theme of middle adolescence—the resurgence of the oedipus complex and the beginning of its resolution. At the same time, we see the continuing struggle in relation to the powerful preoedipal bond with mother. The ties with both parents become modulated in intensity as Anne becomes aware of new sexual feelings stirring within herself and falls in love for the first time. Through the pages of the diary, we may trace the role of this relationship in allowing a beginning resolution of the conflicts of middle adolescence.

In Anne's diary we have a classic statement of the revival of oedipal passions. She adores her father and cannot abide her mother. She is jealous, too, of any other women in his life. When the coquettish Mrs. Van Daan flirts with him, "pulling her skirt right up, making so-called witty remarks," Anne cannot contain herself and rebukes her sharply. When her father is affectionate toward her sister, this, too, makes her jealous:

> I love them; but only because they are Mummy and Margot. With Daddy it's different. If he holds Margot up as an example, approves of what she does, praises and caresses her, then something gnaws at me inside, because I adore Daddy. He is the one I look up to. I don't love anyone in the world but him.

The passage concludes, "I want something from Daddy that he is not able to give me. . . . I long for Daddy's real love: not only as his child, but for me—Anne, myself" ([13 yrs., 4 mos.] p. 40).

The examples could be multiplied: "Mummy gave me another frightful sermon this morning: I can't bear them. Our ideas are completely opposite. Daddy is a darling, although he can sometimes be angry with me for five minutes on end" ([13 yrs., 2 mos.] p. 23). "Just had a big bust-up with Mummy for the umpteenth time; we simply don't get on together these days. . . . Margot's and Mummy's natures are completely strange to me. . . . If Daddy wasn't so patient, I'd be afraid I was going to turn out to be a terrific disappointment to my parents" ([13 yrs., 2 mos.] p. 27). "We [she and her mother] are exact opposites in everything; so naturally we are bound to run up against each other" ([13 yrs., 4 mos.] p. 41). Anne is certain that she herself would be a more compatible and responsive wife than her mother.

She indeed shares a great deal with her father and feels loved by him, if not in the way she would now wish. They study English together, puzzle over mathematics, discuss books. On the second Christmas in hiding, when there is nothing left to give, they work together to compose a little poem for each person, which they place in the person's shoe. But when Anne tries to enlist him in an alliance against her mother, he gently turns aside her efforts. He understands what Anne cannot—that the intensity of her feelings toward him will resolve in time:

> There was another dust-up yesterday. Mummy kicked up a frightful row and told Daddy just what she thought of me. Then she had an awful fit of tears so, of course, off I went too; and I'd got such an awful headache anyway. Finally I told Daddy that I'm much more fond of him than Mummy, to which he replied that I'd get over that. But I don't believe it. [(13 yrs., 3 mos.) p. 34]

In the early part of the diary, Anne's entries about her mother are a litany of accusations. Even when her mother does something that Anne might be expected to welcome, it becomes merely the occasion for sarcasm: "Dear Kitty, May I introduce someone to you: Mama Frank, champion of youth! Extra butter for the young; the problems of modern youth; Mummy defends youth in everything and after a certain amount of squabbling she always gets her way" ([13 yrs., 9 mos.] p. 63). Continuing in the same paragraph, Anne's next thought, seemingly unrelated, concerns the two cats who had shared the premises they now occupy, who, whenever they met, always had "a terrific fight." This is indeed the state of things between Anne and her mother: they have just had their "umpteenth row," they have just had a "frightful dust-up." In this volatile atmosphere, almost anything suffices to set off an explosion.

Again and again, Anne returns to her disappointment in her mother for having ceased to be the idealized figure of her childhood imagination. "I have in my mind's eye an image of what a perfect mother and wife should be; and in her whom I must call 'Mother' I find no trace of that image." In an effort at exorcism, Anne denies her mother's influence, denies her own identification with her, denies her very maternity: "I have to be my own mother. I've drawn myself apart from them all; I am my own skipper and later on I shall see where I come to land. . . . I must become good through my own efforts, without examples and without good advice" ([13 yrs., 4 mos.] p. 41).

In the early portions of the diary, Anne's statements about her mother are of a piece: they are unremittingly critical. There comes a point, though, when she steps back and reflects upon her own feelings. Reading over what she has written in her diary, she is "shocked" to see how consistently her entries about her mother were "brimful of rage" and "filled with hate." She admits for the first time that her mother has some redeeming qualities, and that she herself has contributed to the volatile state that exists between them:

> I used to be furious with Mummy, and still am sometimes. It's true that she doesn't understand me, but I don't understand her either. She did love me very much and she was tender, but as she landed in so many unpleasant situations through me, and was nervous and irritable because of other worries and difficulties, it is certainly understandable that she snapped at me.
>
> I took it much too seriously, was offended, and was rude and

aggravating to Mummy, which, in turn, made her unhappy. So it was really a matter of unpleasantness and misery rebounding all the time. It wasn't nice for either of us, but it is passing. [(14 yrs., 6 mos.) pp. 114–15]

Here Anne rescinds her retrospective distortion—her belief that things had always been this way—and acknowledges that things have been otherwise in the past, and may be otherwise in the future. She expresses remorse for the feelings she has harbored, and ends by consoling herself that it is better that her "hard words be on paper than that Mummy should carry them in her heart."

How can this sudden change be understood? To examine its context, I turn back the pages of the diary to see what preceded her present state of feeling. In the previous entry, Anne had written of her grandmother, who is now dead: "Granny, oh, darling Granny, how little we understood of what she suffered, or how sweet she was. . . . How faithful and good Granny always was; she would never have let one of us down. Whatever it was, however naughty I had been, Granny always stuck up for me" ([14 yrs., 6 mos.] p. 113). Continuing in the same tone, Anne's thoughts then turn to her friend Lies, who she believes may also be dead. Realizing that the fate she imagines for her friend might have been her own, Anne accuses herself of being selfish and cowardly, undeserving of what God has given her. As her thoughts are drawn to the losses of two important female figures, Anne feels deeply guilty toward both; in this context, she suddenly becomes frightened by the intensity of her anger at her mother. The fulfillment of her angry wishes was all too real a possibility.

But by the next entry, written just a few days later, Anne has returned to her litany of reproaches. She dredges up an old grievance she has been harboring and meditates further upon her mother's shortcomings. Once again she measures her against an imaginary ideal, and again finds her lacking ("I imagine a mother as a woman who, in the first place . . .").

Why does Anne need so quickly to reinstate her position as angry critic of her mother? Again, the sequence of her thoughts and feelings is revealing. The renewed criticism of her mother comes in an entry which she begins by telling Kitty, "I have two things to *confess* to you today" (my emphasis). The first is about her mother—and Anne goes on to set forth her grievances. The second, she writes, is "very difficult to tell you, because it is about myself." It is about the welling up of sexual feeling. She introduces the subject by mentioning an article she had been reading, in which the author writes about a girl's awareness of the changes of puberty. Anne comments, "I experience that, too, and that is why I get the feeling lately of being embarrassed about Margot, Mummy, and Daddy." Thus, she intuits that there is a connection between the maturation of her body and the need to draw back from her family.

Anne speaks with pleasure about the bodily changes she is experiencing, and then continues:

> Sometimes, when I lie in bed at night, I have a terrible desire to feel my breasts and to listen to the quiet rhythmic beat of my heart.
>
> I already had these kinds of feelings subconsciously before I came here, because I remember that once when I slept with a girl friend I had a strong desire to kiss her, and that I did so. I could not help being terribly inquisitive over her body, for she had always kept it hidden from me. I asked whether, as proof of our friendship, we should feel one another's breasts, but she refused. I go into ecstasies every time I see the naked figure of a woman, such as Venus, for example. It strikes me as so wonderful and exquisite that I have difficulty in stopping the tears rolling down my cheeks.
>
> If only I had a girl friend! [(14 yrs., 6 mos.) pp. 116–17]

The onset of adolescent sexuality has rarely found such sensitive expression. The passage marks a turning point in the diary and in Anne's development.

What engages our attention is that the sexual longings Anne "confesses" to Kitty are focused upon the very symbol of mother—breasts. These are the object of both her masturbatory and homosexual impulses. Her thoughts turn next to Venus, whose naked figure is so exquisite that Anne has difficulty in stopping herself from weeping. Reading of the powerful effect of this eternally idealized woman, we are reminded of her assertions, repeated insistently, of how far her own mother is from the ideal.

The present diary entry, with its immediate connection between the two "confessions," suggests that Anne's anger at her mother, which returns here in full force, is not only the jealousy of the oedipal rival. The anger is invoked defensively. It is an attempt to free herself from a bond which, with the welling up of adult impulses, is experienced as having homosexual overtones. The two "confessions" that Anne juxtaposes are related. The first, the renewal of her anger against her mother, is an attempt to ward off what nonetheless emerges—the homosexual longing that constitutes her second "confession."

Anne's description, still in the same diary entry, of her response to the changes in her body is an extraordinary passage. Reading it, one forgets the harrowing circumstances in which it was written and Anne's ultimate fate. Rather, the reader is drawn into Anne's inner world:

> The second [confession] is something that is very difficult to tell you, because it is about myself.
>
> Yesterday I read an article about blushing by Sis Heyster. This article might have been addressed to me personally. Although I don't blush very easily, the other things in it certainly all fit me. She writes roughly something like this—that a girl in the years of puberty becomes quiet within and begins to think about the wonders that are happening to her body.
>
> I experience that, too. . . .
>
> I think that what is happening to me is so wonderful, and not only what can be seen on my body, but all that is taking place inside. I never discuss myself or any of these things with anybody; that is why I have to talk to myself about them.
>
> Each time I have a period—and that has only been three times— I have the feeling that in spite of all the pain, unpleasantness, and nastiness, I have a sweet secret, and that is why, although it is nothing but a nuisance to me in a way, I always long for the time that I shall feel that secret within me again. [(14 yrs., 6 mos.) p. 117]

The passage is a quiet hymn of joy in her approaching womanhood.

Its tone contrasts with that of most psychoanalytic writing about the girl's experience, which has emphasized the negative impact of menarche—its regressive and anxiety-arousing aspects.[3] Anne's diary brings

---

3. Deutsch (1944), who devoted a chapter of *The Psychology of Women* to the subject, delineated a multiplicity of possible meanings the event may have for the girl, then summarized her observations, "The first menstruation is usually experienced as a trauma" (vol. 1, p. 157). More recent statements (e.g., Harley, 1971; Ritvo, 1976) have often preserved this emphasis, linking menstruation to earlier fantasies of castration, to punishment for masturbation, to excretory phenomena on the model of urinary and anal functions. An exception is Kestenberg (1961), who finds that the onset of menstruation brings greater clarity both to the girl's body image and thought processes. In this context, see also Hart and Sarnoff (1971); Shopper (1979).

to our attention another aspect of this complex event. She describes menstruation as a "sweet secret" which she longs to feel again. Her statement, of course, represents conscious experience rather than unconscious fantasy as it is revealed, over time, in the psychoanalytic situation. But the diary offers another kind of evidence, one that is less subject to conscious control: that is the language Anne uses. The imagery that now begins to appear in her writing about herself suggests that the onset of menstruation is associated with a profound change both in the mental representation of her body and in her self-representation.

This change is first suggested in the passage about her response to the maturation of her body. I have already quoted the passage in full but repeat parts of it here, with emphasis added: "a girl in the years of puberty becomes *quiet within*. . . . I think that what is happening to me is so wonderful, and not only what can be seen on my body, but all that is *taking place inside*. . . . I always long for the time that I shall feel *that secret within me* again" (pp. 116–17). It is clear that Anne has now begun to have an increased awareness of the inside of her body. In the weeks and months that follow, Anne describes the welling up of sexual feeling. I shall trace this theme in detail, but in the present context I wish simply to note the terms in which it is expressed: "I believe that it's spring within me. . . ." Peter "kept on looking too and then—yes, then—it gave me a lovely feeling inside, but which I mustn't feel too often." ". . . he gave me such a gentle warm look which made a tender glow within me." "If he looks at me with those eyes that laugh and wink, then it's as if a little light goes on inside me." And listening to Mozart with Peter, "I can hardly listen in the room because I'm always so inwardly stirred when I hear lovely music."

The new sense of "within" is apparent not only in sexual contexts. It permeates the imagery Anne now uses to write of her changing sense of self. After a year and a half in the secret annexe, in a long reflection on her own development, Anne observes that she was a different person during her school days from the Anne who has "grown wise within these walls." She contrasts her earlier self, always looking outward, to her present self, sensing what is within. Now she has "discovered my inward happiness and my defensive armor of superficiality and gaiety." The recurrent metaphors have to do with outside and inside. It is in these terms, too, that she writes of her growth toward womanhood: "I know that I'm a woman, a woman with inward strength." A month later she writes, "Every day I feel that I am developing inwardly." And in what would be the final entry of the diary, the same imagery recurs. Here Anne writes of herself as having a lighthearted outer self and a more serious inner self, a "deeper Anne."

> I know exactly how I'd like to be, how I am too . . . inside. But alas, I'm only that for myself. And perhaps that's why, no, I'm sure it's the reason why I say I've got a happy nature within and why other people think I've got a happy nature without. I am guided by the pure Anne within, and outside I'm nothing but a frolicsome little goat who's broken loose. [(15 yrs., 1 mo.) p. 240]

The language of "inside/outside," of which there are abundant examples in the latter part of Anne's diary, rarely appears in the earlier sections. After the time when Anne writes of having begun menstruating and of longing to feel that "sweet secret" again, subsequent entries in the diary reflect in multiple ways an increased sense of "within."

With the beginning of menstruation, the girl has the first tangible evidence of—the first "contact" with—her unseen, unfelt uterus. We may regard menarche as one in a series of critical experiences that successively articulate for the female the *subjective reality* of her inner sexual and reproductive organs. What we see in Anne's diary is the beginning of a profound alteration in the mental representation of the body, and concomitantly in her self-representation, which is manifest in a shift in the very language she uses.

In the diary, the onset of menstruation is associated with the first stirring of sexual feeling. It is after writing of having begun to menstruate that Anne goes on to describe the wish to feel her own breasts and those of a friend. This passage ends with the cry, "If only I had a girl friend!" It is an unanswerable question whether, at this point, had Anne been living in ordinary circumstances she would have formed a homo-sexually tinged friendship of the sort characteristic of early adolescence. As it was, the only person close to her own age, outside her family, with whom Anne had contact was Peter Van Daan. It is to Peter, now, that Anne turns.

It was later that same day—the day that Anne wrote of her sexual longings—that she found an excuse to spend time alone with Peter. She offered to help him with his crossword puzzles, and she records that they sat opposite each other at his table, he on the chair and she on the divan. Here is her account of their time together:

It gave me a queer feeling each time I looked into his deep blue
eyes, and he sat there with that mysterious laugh playing round his
lips. . . . I could see on his face that look of helplessness and un-
certainty as to how to behave, and, at the same time, a trace of
his sense of manhood. I noticed his shy manner and it made me
feel very gentle; I couldn't refrain from meeting those dark eyes
again and again. [(14 yrs., 6 mos.) p. 118]

Compare this with Anne's first impression of Peter when the Van Daans
arrived at the secret annexe: "a rather soft, shy, gawky youth; can't
expect much from his company." Her opinion had not improved much
a week later: "I still don't like Peter any more, he is so boring; he flops
lazily on his bed half the time, does a bit of carpentry, and then goes
back for another snooze! What a fool!"

Now, after describing the extended visit with Peter, Anne tells Kitty
that she thought about him as she lay in bed that night. She quickly
adds, "Whatever you do, don't think I'm in love with Peter—not a bit
of it!" She then goes on to describe a dream she had that very night
about Peter—not this Peter, but another who is safely absent, Peter
Wessel:

I woke at about five to seven this morning and knew at once, quite
positively, what I had dreamed. I sat on a chair and opposite me
sat Peter . . . Wessel. We were looking together at a book of drawings by Mary Bos. The dream was so vivid that I can still partly
remember the drawings. But that was not all—the dream went
on. Suddenly Peter's eyes met mine and I looked into those fine,
velvet brown eyes for a long time. Then Peter said very softly, "If
I had only known, I would have come to you long before!" I turned
around brusquely because the emotion was too much for me. And
after that I felt a soft, and oh, such a cool kind cheek against mine
and it felt so good, so good. . . .

I awoke at this point, while I could still feel his cheek against
mine and felt his brown eyes looking deep into my heart, so deep,
that there he read how much I had loved him and how much I
still love him. [(14 yrs., 6 mos.) p. 119]

Anne's punctuation—the ellipses after "Peter" are hers—marks the
ambiguity of the name in her dream. (Significantly, the ellipses after "it
felt so good, so good" are also hers.) In its manifest content, the dream

simply transposes Anne's experience with Peter Van Daan that afternoon: she and "Peter" are sitting opposite one another, engaged in a bookish activity, and their eyes meet in a way that is sexually exciting. In the dream, Anne wishes that their contact had gone further, that she had felt his cheek against her own, that he had penetrated deep inside her, with his eyes.

In the balance of this entry and in the next, we have some of Anne's associations to her dream. She goes on to write that the image of Peter reminds her of three other dream images that were equally vivid. The first is of her paternal grandmother, whom she "saw so clearly one night that I could even distinguish her thick, soft, wrinkled velvety skin." The second is of her maternal grandmother, who "appeared as a guardian angel." The third is of her friend Lies, "a symbol to me of the suffering of all my girl friends and all Jews."

The three figures with whom Peter is linked in Anne's associations are important people whom she has loved—significantly, all female. The first two, her grandmothers, are obviously maternal figures. Of these, the first is seen so close up—"I could even distinguish her thick, soft, winkled velvety skin"—that the image is not so much visual as tactile, like the infant's earliest experience of the mother. The second maternal figure is experienced as magically protective and omnipotent. The third in the series is Anne's best friend, Lies, with whom, as we know, she had had a conflictual relationship over time. Earlier Anne had felt that Lies abandoned her; now she feels she is the abandoning one, living safely while Lies may be dead. Theirs was a relationship marked not only by warmth but by jealousy, anger, and guilt.

All three of these females may be considered to be aspects of the maternal imago. Indeed, their ordering recalls a developmental sequence. The first two suggest the omnipotent, magically protective mother of the infant's earliest experience; the third, the mother of subsequent separation, inevitably the object of intense ambivalence. As Anne begins to fall in love, the associations to her dream would seem to recall the antecedents of this relationship. They recall the powerful preoedipal bond with her mother to which this new attachment becomes, in part, the heir.

The inclusion of both grandmothers links Anne's feeling for Peter not only with her mother, but also with her father. It will be recalled that Peter Wessel had been mentioned in the first pages of the diary, in Anne's description of her birthday party. The context in which he then appeared was of Anne's successfully keeping secret from her mother her plan of marrying him. Now Anne gives us more information about this young man. He was tall and handsome, older than she: although they were "inseparable for one whole summer," he later gave her up because he saw her as "a childish little imp." Instead, he "went around with girls of his own age and didn't even think of saying 'Hello' to me any more; but I—couldn't forget him" and "I never fell in love again." Anne was intensely jealous of these older girls. Boys her own age took an interest in her, but she could not reciprocate their feeling. Rather, "as I grew older and more mature my love grew with me. I can quite understand now that Peter thought me childish, and yet it still hurt" ([14 yrs., 6 mos.] p. 127). Her words convey the pain of oedipal longing.

Thus, the absent "Peter Wessel" of Anne's dream is a condensation. First and most obviously, he is the object of sexual feelings Anne is beginning to have toward his namesake, Peter Van Daan. Beyond this, however, her associations to the dream link him with each of her parents and suggest that he inherits her intense feeling for both of them. Anne's relationship with Peter reproduces, in some ways, these familial ties at the same time that it allows her to begin the process of intrapsychic separation from each of her parents.

Anne herself sees the dream as a turning point. In the days following, her fantasies center on the absent Peter of the dream, but his image is soon displaced by the real Peter of the present. Not long after their extended visit in his room, Anne begins an entry in her diary, "Something has happened to me." The event—she realizes she can hardly call it that, yet it seems momentous—is a conversation with Peter. As he, Margot, and Anne were peeling potatoes, the conversation turned to the resident cat, and it was Anne who raised the question whether it was male or female. Peter offered to show her, an offer she immediately took up ("I couldn't control my curiosity"). Here, for the first time, the shy, passive Peter assumes the role of authority. He turned the cat on his back, "deftly held his head and paws together, and the lesson began. 'Those are male organs, these are just a few stray hairs, and that is his bottom.'" Anne is impressed by Peter's matter-of-factness; after this demonstration of his expertise, she begins to see him in a different light.

It is not long before Anne realizes, "Kitty, I'm just like someone in love who can only talk about her darling. And Peter really is a darling!" She is indeed just like someone in love: "From early in the morning till late at night, I really do hardly anything else but think of Peter. I sleep with his image before my eyes, dream about him and he is still looking at me when I awake" ([14 yrs., 8 mo.] p. 144). Over the next weeks and months, Anne records in minute detail all of their contacts—each of their conversations, each of their passings on the stairs. Mundane events become imbued with great feeling. She confides to her diary:

> He gave me such a gentle warm look which made a tender glow within me. I could really see that he wanted to please me, and because he couldn't make a long complimentary speech he spoke with his eyes. I understood him, oh, so well, and was very grateful. It gives me pleasure even now when I recall those words and that look. [(14 yrs., 8 mos.) p. 139]

The occasion for this pleasure and gratitude—the cause of the "tender glow"—was Peter's having congratulated her on finding the very smallest potatoes to give Margot for her birthday.

Like any teenager in love, Anne finds herself suddenly bursting into tears, thinking that perhaps Peter doesn't like her at all, or only thinks of her casually. The mood swings, the excitement, the restlessness, the exhilaration—all the characteristic passion of first love is recorded here: "I believe that it's spring within me, I feel that spring is awakening, I feel it in my whole body and soul. It is an effort to behave normally, I feel utterly confused, don't know what to read, what to write, what to do, I only know that I am longing. . . !" ([14 yrs., 8 mos.] p. 136)

Anne Frank's diary stands as a timeless description of how it feels to fall in love for the first time. Like many young lovers, Anne and Peter discover nature—even though they were unable to go out of doors:

> Is there anything more beautiful in the world than to sit before an open window and enjoy nature, to listen to the birds singing, feel the sun on your cheeks and have a darling boy in your arms? It is so soothing and peaceful to feel his arms around me, to know that he is close by and yet to remain silent, it can't be bad, for this tranquility is good. [(14 yrs., 10 mos.) pp. 192–93]

The weeks go by and Anne breathlessly records their first kiss. Her excitement spilling over everywhere, she addresses this entry "Darlingest Kitty" and implores her to remember yesterday's date, "for it is a very important day in my life." She and Peter were sitting close together:

> Oh, it was so lovely, I couldn't talk much, the joy was too great.

He stroked my cheek and arm a bit awkwardly, played with my curls and our heads lay touching most of the time, I can't tell you, Kitty, the feeling that ran through me all the while. . . .

How it came about so suddenly, I don't know, but before we went downstairs he kissed me, through my hair, half on my cheek, half on my ear; I tore downstairs without looking around, and am simply longing for today! [(14 yrs., 10 mos.) p.190]

Anne begins the next diary entry, "Do you think that Daddy and Mummy would approve of my sitting and kissing a boy on a divan—a boy of 17½ and a girl of just under 15?"

All along, her parents have been an insistent internal presence. The morning after her dream about Peter, Anne had written, "When Daddy kissed me this morning, I could have cried out, 'Oh, if only you were Peter!' " It is the first of many associative links between the two: "Peter is a first-rate chap, too, just like Daddy!" And as her father reads aloud from Dickens, "I was in seventh heaven, because I sat on Daddy's chair very close to Peter." Later, she will assure this young man, "I do trust you, Peter, just as much as I trust Daddy." Anne's adolescent love for Peter is heir to the young girl's admiration for her father: "I like it much better if he explains something to me than when I have to teach him; I would really adore him to be my superior in almost everything."

But if Anne's feeling for Peter bears the unmistakable stamp of oedipal love, it also bears the imprint of her earlier love for her mother. She turns to him with needs whose earliest satisfaction had been in this relationship; her physical yearning is in part the yearning for comfort that the child finds in the mother's body. The lovers retreat to the attic, where before an open window they "recapture happiness," in Anne's words, through the sense of oneness with nature and each other, silently sharing the "overwhelming feeling of bliss." It is essential, she writes, that "the spell should not be broken by words." To do so would destroy the momentary recapturing of a preverbal period of life.

There is relief and exhilaration in the breaking down of boundaries; the sense of separateness is alleviated as each finds in the other a reflection of the self. Anne discovers that "Peter and I are really not so different as we would appear to be" ([14 yrs. 8 mos.] p.144). The reason is that "we both lack a mother." His is too superficial, while hers lacks "real motherliness." Both "wrestle with our inner feelings, we are still uncertain and are really too sensitive to be roughly treated." When they are hurt, Anne acts noisy and boisterous, while Peter withdraws into silence. Anne now finds, however, that these are simply different ways of concealing their true selves. They both lack mothers, she writes. In turning to one another, I am suggesting, each attempts to make restitution for what is now missing.

Several weeks after this entry, Anne describes what she calls "the most wonderful evening I have ever had in the 'Secret Annexe.' " Sitting together in semidarkness before an open window, she and Peter spoke of the estrangement between themselves and their parents:

> We talked about how neither of us could confide in our parents, and how his parents would have loved to have his confidence, but that he didn't wish it. How I cry my heart out in bed, and he goes up to the loft and swears. . . . Over every imaginable thing—oh, he was just as I thought!" [(14 yrs., 9 mos.) p. 162]

They confess their initial impressions of one another, how in the beginning each couldn't bear the other. Throughout, the repeated theme is the contrast between initially having felt that they were so different, and now feeling that they are the same. In this diary entry, as in others with this theme, the final association is to sexual longing—through which the yearning for fusion finds adult expression.

If Anne's love for Peter is shaped by her earlier relations with each of her parents, it is, at the same time, integral in the process of disengagement from them. Anne's withdrawal from her father is a slow, steady undercurrent beneath the surface of her passionate preoccupation with Peter. On the morning after her dream, when her father came to kiss her, Anne could hardly keep from exclaiming, "Oh, if only you were Peter!" And as time goes on, she finds that when she allows her eyes to meet Peter's, it gives her "a lovely feeling inside, but which I mustn't feel too often." Where, next, do her thoughts turn? "Daddy has noticed that I'm not quite my usual self, but I really can't tell him everything. 'Leave me in peace, leave me alone,' that's what I'd like to keep crying out all the time."

Anne now finds her parents irritating. More than a year has passed since she wrote, "I adore Daddy. . . . I don't love anyone in the world but him." Compare with this her present tone: "Mummy is tiresome, Daddy sweet and therefore all the more tiresome. . . ." She resents always being asked what she is going to do when she is on her way to Peter's room. She complains that every book she reads must be inspected—

although she immediately acknowledges that her parents are not at all strict. "Something else, especially about me, that doesn't please them: I don't feel like giving them lots of kisses any more. . . . In short, I'd really like to be rid of them for a while" [(14 yrs., 9 mos.) p. 161].

Rid of "them": in the early portions of the diary, her parents had always been "Mummy" and "Daddy," separate and contrasted. As Anne's love for Peter allows her to extricate herself from oedipal passions, she can again tolerate seeing her parents as a couple. Often, they are lumped together with the other adults in the secret annexe as the older generation: "Have the two sets of parents forgotten their own youth?" "Us" and "them" are no longer me/Daddy vs. Margot/Mummy. Now the lines separate the generations: "Everything is all right again, except that Margot and I are getting a bit tired of our parents. . . . When you are as old as we are, you want to decide a few things for yourself, you want to be independent sometimes" ([14 yrs., 9 mos.] p. 161). The relationship with Peter not only allows Anne to relinquish her father to her mother, she now "gives" him to her other rival, Margot. Anne makes this gesture in a letter to her sister in which she expresses concern lest Margot be jealous of her relationship with Peter. Margot assures her that she is not: she could only be intimate with someone who was her intellectual superior, and this she could never feel with Peter. But such, she imagines, *would* be the case with Anne and Peter.

As Anne has been impelled into the relationship with Peter in part because of the anxiety that now invades the ties to her parents, so she seeks refuge in these ties when her deepening intimacy with Peter presents its own dangers. She becomes frightened by the possibility of acting on her sexual impulses. This conflict had been present from the first. Reflecting on the dream about Peter Wessel with its accompanying sexual excitement, Anne had exclaimed, "I love him with all my heart and soul. I give myself completely!" She immediately added, however, a cautionary note: "But one thing, he may touch my face, but no more."

Anne is aware of the internal conflict, which she describes as "a war that reigns incessantly within—a war between desire and common sense." After Peter kissed her for the first time, she "tore downstairs without looking round"—then couldn't wait to see him again. In her diary the next day, she espouses in turn each side of her conflict. First, she projects onto a succession of other females the disapproval she herself feels:

I know almost for certain that Margot would never kiss a boy unless there had been some talk of an engagement or marriage. . . . I'm sure that Mummy never touched a man before Daddy. What would my girl friends say about it if they knew that I lay in Peter's arms, my heart against his chest, my head on his shoulder and with his head against mine!

She then goes on to argue against their imagined disapproval:

Oh, Anne, how scandalous! But honestly, I don't think it is; we are shut up here, shut away from the world, in fear and anxiety, especially just lately. Why, then, should we who love each other remain apart? Why should we wait until we've reached a suitable age? . . . Why shouldn't I follow the way my heart leads me, if it makes us both happy? [(14 yrs., 10 mos.) p. 191]

Finally, Anne acknowledges the ambivalence as her own, and asks the imaginary Kitty to advise her: "Do you think it's my duty to tell Daddy what I'm doing?"

As the kisses become more passionate, her conflict is intensified:

Once more there is a question which gives me no peace: "Is it right? Is it right that I should have yielded so soon, that I am so ardent, just as ardent and eager as Peter himself? May I, a girl, let myself go to this extent?" . . . I am afraid of myself, I am afraid that in my longing I am giving myself too quickly. [(14 yrs., 10 mos.) pp. 196–97]

As after the first shy kiss, the next entry in the diary begins with the thought of telling her father. This time it is Peter to whom she attributes her wish: "After some discussion, he came to the conclusion that I should." She then takes the earliest opportunity to inform her father: "Daddy, I expect you've gathered that when we're together Peter and I don't sit miles apart. Do you think it's wrong?"

As is characteristic of adolescents, Anne has found a way of externalizing the conflict which, until now, had been internal. Predictably, her father tells her not to spend so much time alone with Peter. This allows Anne to espouse the other side of her ambivalence. In defiance of her father's request that she not go to Peter's room, she declares emphatically to Kitty, "No, I'm going!"

The "war that reigns incessantly within" is no longer within: now it is between Anne and her father, each expressing an aspect of Anne's own conflict. By informing her father, she has drawn the lines of battle between them. At the same time, she has succeeded in reengaging him in her intimate concerns, calling upon him to be once more the authoritative and protective father of childhood.

After he has asked Anne not to spend so much time alone with Peter, she sends her father a letter of accusation and reproach. It concludes, "I have now reached the stage that I can live entirely on my own. . . . I shall not be sorry for what I have done, but shall act as I think I can. You can't coax me into not going upstairs; *either* you forbid it, or you trust me through thick and thin, but then leave me in peace as well!" ([14 yrs., 10 mos.] p. 203). While asserting her independence, Anne is all but imploring her father to make his prohibition more strict. By delegating to him aspects of her superego, Anne has attempted to free herself from internal conflict. With her father on the side of prohibition, she can safely be on the side of impulse.

But the rift itself alarms her. She is distressed to see how upset her father is by her letter, which he perceptively summarizes as meaning that Anne feels wronged and deserted. Anne becomes frightened not only by the possibility of acting on her sexual impulses, but by the distance she has created between herself and her father. Remorseful, Anne now rescinds the sentiments she expressed in the letter.

The effect of Anne's reproachful letter, finally, is to bring about a rapprochement with her father. Frightened, she now retreats once more into her family. In the next diary entry, she decides to fill in details of her family background, going back to the childhood of each of her parents. In the one following, we hear echoes of the childlike tone of the early pages of the diary. She has finished a story and copied it out onto nice paper, and while it certainly looks very attractive, "Is it really enough for Daddy's birthday?" The rapprochement with her father is accompanied by an increasing disillusionment with Peter: "He's a darling, but I soon closed up my inner self from him. If he wants to force the lock again he'll have to work a good deal harder than before!" And a week later, "Peter is good and he's a darling, but still there's no denying that there's a lot about him that disappoints me." He all but disappears from her diary at this point.

Having lost interest in Peter, Anne throws herself into intellectual pursuits with consuming intensity:

Dear Kitty,

I'm frightfully busy at the moment, and although it sounds mad, I haven't time to get through my pile of work. Shall I tell you briefly what I have got to do? Well, then, by tomorrow I must finish reading the first part of *Galileo Galilei,* as it has to be returned to the library. I only started it yesterday, but I shall manage it.

Next week I have got to read *Palestine at the Crossroads* and the second part of *Galilei*. Next I finished reading the first part of the biography of *The Emperor Charles V* yesterday, and it's essential that I work out all the diagrams and family trees that I have collected from it. After that I have three pages of foreign words gathered from various books, which have all got to be recited, written down, and learned. Number four is that my film stars are all mixed up together and are simply gasping to be tidied up; however, as such a clearance would take several days, and since Professor Anne, as she's already said, is choked with work, the chaos will have to remain a chaos.

Next Theseus, Oedipus, Peleus, Orpheus, Jason, and Hercules are all awaiting their turn to be arranged, as their different deeds lie crisscross in my mind like fancy threads in a dress; it's also high time Myron and Phidias had some treatment, if they wish to remain at all coherent. Likewise it's the same with the seven and nine years' war; I'm mixing everything up together at this rate. Yes, but what can one do with such a memory! Think how forgetful I shall be when I'm eighty! [(14 yrs., 10 mos.) p. 209]

The passage is a charming example of the adaptive use of intellectuality as a defense in adolescence. We see the transparent guise in which the repressed returns, however, as Anne goes on to detail her biblical interests: "How long is it still going to take before I meet the bathing Susanna? And what do they mean by the guilt of Sodom and Gomorrah? Oh, there is still such a terrible lot to find out and learn." The bathing Susanna, it will be recalled, is a young girl whose nakedness is being admired by old men.

The interests that come tumbling out in this breathless passage suggest, first, Anne's need to reorder her life, to reassert control after being swept away by impulse. Beyond this, her agenda reflects the search for new figures to occupy the place once filled by the idealized parents of childhood. Like many adolescents, Anne looks elsewhere to find larger-than-life heroes and heroines to replace her parents. She is fascinated by the genealogy of the various royal families of Europe, and spends hours working out their family trees. She is also interested in mythology and reads eagerly about the gods and goddesses of the ancient world. The gods and goddesses of the modern world are of no less interest: she pores over her collection of pictures of film stars, and reads movie magazines so devotedly that her mother jokes that once they leave the secret annexe Anne won't have to see the movies they have missed— she already knows all about them from her reading. These interests were in abeyance, for a time, while Peter assumed heroic proportions. As he is diminished in her estimation, Anne returns with renewed passion to her old interest in celebrities, deities, and royalty.

Her own parents could never again be what they had seemed to her in childhood. Although Anne seeks a rapprochement with her father, it is not a return to an earlier state. Anne's relationship with each of her parents has been irrevocably altered by her "first love." She says little, in the final entries, of her mother: she has less need to rail against her, less need to repudiate her because their bond is now less frightening. In one of the last entries, Anne says of her parents—now collectively— that "they have always thoroughly spoiled me, were sweet to me, defended me, and have done all that parents could do." Toward her father she remains affectionate, but she can no longer "share secret thoughts" with him. Finally, she finds his "affectionate ways" irritating and would really prefer that he leave her in peace for a while.

Much has changed within Anne over the past two years. The awakening of sexual feeling and falling in love have brought about a profound change not only in her relationships with her parents, but in her sense of self. Even within the confines of the secret annexe, we see the familiar movement back and forth, during adolescence, between the world outside the family and the family itself. The extrafamilial world offers a refuge from the conflict that, with the onset of puberty, invades the bonds with parents; at the same time, the family becomes a refuge from the anxieties aroused in new relationships. It is this repeated movement back and forth that ultimately brings about, under normal circumstances, a new achievement of individuality and autonomy.

III

At the age of thirteen, as her family prepared to go into hiding, Anne hurriedly stuffed into a school satchel her "most vital belongings"—the first of which was her diary. Why was the diary of such critical importance at this time? Anne herself suggests part of the answer to this question, and in pressing this inquiry further, I shall attempt to explore the developmental significance of the diary itself.

After the diary, Anne took "hair curlers, handkerchiefs, schoolbooks, a comb, old letters; I put in the craziest things with the idea that we were going into hiding." Her own comment on the things she chose to bring with her was that "I'm not sorry, memories mean more to me than dresses." Anne was leaving all that had been familiar in the past, with the future entirely unknowable. She was surrounded by death and destruction on an unprecedented scale. In the face of these losses, her most urgent need was to preserve. And what she wished to preserve was not possessions but the past itself—memories. This the diary par excellence allows the writer to do, for it records not simply the outward event, like a photograph, but the inner experience. At a time of loss, the diary assumes crucial importance because it is a means of preserving, and thus of staving off the full affect associated with loss.

On the day she was given the diary, Anne had written the following inscription on its opening page: "I hope I shall be able to confide in you completely, as I have never been able to do in anyone before, and I hope that you will be a great support and comfort to me." From the outset, then, the diary is imagined as an "other" with whom a relationship is to develop. The fantasy is explained and elaborated as Anne reflects further upon her reasons for beginning a diary. The first is the wish, as she puts it, to "bring out all kinds of things that lie buried in my heart." She recalls, in this context, an adage, "Paper is more patient than man," by which she means that in the diary she will not be criticized for what she reveals. But she comes, finally, to what she considers "the root of the matter, the reason for my starting a diary." This is that she feels she has no real friends. She adds immediately that the subjective feeling does not match the external description of her life. "I have darling parents and a sister of sixteen. I know about thirty people whom one might call friends—I have strings of boy friends, anxious to catch a glimpse of me. . . ." In spite of this, however, there is no one with whom she feels as close as she would wish. "Hence, this diary. . . . I don't want to set down a series of bald facts in a diary like most people do, but *I want this diary itself to be my friend,* and I shall call my friend Kitty" (emphasis added).

Anne's reflections on starting a diary at the age of thirteen begin to suggest the multiplicity of functions it serves. She indicates, first, the simplest of these: there is a need to express hidden thoughts and feelings. In the diary this may be done without fear of criticism. Furthermore, what is expressed in the diary will nonetheless remain private; as Anne observes, Kitty is well able to keep a secret. Thus, the diary allows the adolescent to reveal herself with relative freedom. It is this which makes it a uniquely rich source of information about the inner life of adolescents.

But to say that the adolescent "reveals herself" does not accurately convey the subjective experience: Anne's words are that she wishes to "confide in" the diary. It is not simply a record of impressions, thoughts, feelings, and impulses. The diary is an imagined "other," a fictional presence created by the adolescent and summoned into being each time the diary is addressed, as it customarily is, in the second person. Anne addresses Kitty as if she were an actual person, capable of being surprised by the unexpected, amused by something entertaining, bored by hearing the same things again and again. After a year and a half in hiding, she writes,

> Dear Kitty,
>
> I asked myself this morning whether you don't sometimes feel rather like a cow who has had to chew over all the old pieces of news again and again, and who finally yawns loudly and silently wishes that Anne would occasionally dig up something new.
>
> Alas, I know it's dull for you, but try to put yourself in my place, and imagine how sick I am of the old cows who keep having to be pulled out of the ditch again. [(14 yrs., 7 mos.) p. 130]

"Try to put yourself in my place," Anne says to Kitty—as if Kitty were not already *in* Anne's place. She imagines Kitty as someone other than herself: "Kitty, if only you knew how I sometimes boil over under so many gibes and jeers." The imaginary Kitty is capable of a whole range of affective responses: "You may laugh, but these things are not so simple. . . ." "I expect you will be rather surprised by the fact that. . . ." "Perhaps it would be entertaining to you if. . . ." And again, "There's no need to make you unhappy about it, too, Kitty, just because I am miserable."

I suggested earlier that keeping a diary is a way of staving off the full affect associated with loss: the diary was therefore the first of her "most vital belongings" that Anne brought with her into hiding. I believe that the diary serves this function not only in relation to the overwhelming loss which history forced upon Anne Frank, but also in relation to that sense of loss which is at the heart of normal adolescence, inherent in the painful process of disengagement from the original objects. It is for this reason that diaries are more often kept during adolescence than at any other period of life—and why they are finally abandoned.

In creating an imaginary being into whom she breathes life, the adolescent attempts to fill the void left when the parents no longer hold the place they held in childhood, but new bonds have not yet been consolidated. During this transition, there is often a period of heightened narcissism, when a retreat into the self and into an inner world of fantasy must substitute (in part, and temporarily) for relations in the outer world. Blos (1962) sees the diary as an expression of this transitional state, standing "between daydream and object world, between make-believe and reality" (p. 94). Indeed, the diary is ideally suited to the narcissism and compensatory grandiosity of this phase. It is a unique form of communication in which one has only to speak and never to listen. It is a literary mode whose legitimate subject is the self. It reflects the fluidity of self-esteem in adolescence—the vacillation between self-disparagement and self-aggrandizement—that the diary is valued both because it will guard one's shameful secrets and also because it may one day be published.

The imagined "other" brought to life in the pages of the diary helps to ward off the depression associated with loss. For Anne, the need was heightened by the isolation in which she was forced to live: she turned to Kitty more faithfully, perhaps, than she might have under normal circumstances. In the very first inscription, written the day the diary was given to her, Anne wrote that she hoped it would be "a great support and comfort" to her. Later statements echo this theme. "Writing has made my 'zum Tode betrubt' [depths of despair] go off a bit." And again, "I can shake off everything if I write; my sorrows disappear, my courage is reborn. . . . *I can recapture everything when I write,* my thoughts, my ideals and my fantasies" ([14 yrs., 9 mos.] pp. 177–78, emphasis added). In a period of flux in thought and mood, the diary allows the adolescent to grasp what would otherwise be fleeting, transitory states, to capture something of the inner life and make it permanent.

Yet what is "recaptured" is more than an inner state. In the imaginary relationship with the diary, the adolescent attempts to recapture aspects of the earlier relationship with the parents.[4] I have emphasized how vividly Anne believes in the fiction that "Kitty" is another person. If she is another person, however, she has the unique characteristic of never seeing things differently than Anne does herself. Anne is complaining, as many adolescents do, of being treated one day as a sensible young woman, the next as a silly little goat who doesn't know anything at all. "Oh, so many things bubble up inside me as I lie in bed, having to put up with people I'm fed up with, who always misinterpret my intentions. That's why in the end I always come back to my diary" ([13 yrs.,

4. Anaïs Nin began keeping her now well-known diary when she was eleven. The adolescent portion, written by a girl altogether different from Anne Frank, nonetheless bears similarities in the relationship to the diary as an imagined presence. The diary begins in 1914. It was also a time of war and uprooting, and for the young girl a time of personal loss as well. Her father, a composer and concert pianist, had recently abandoned the family. As she begins keeping a diary, Anaïs, with her mother and two brothers, are leaving Barcelona for America. She later wrote: "The diary began as a diary of a journey, to record everything for my father. It was written for him, and I had intended to send it to him. It was really a letter, so he could follow us into a strange land" (1931–34, p. 202). She copied into the diary her letters to her father; at first, these are full of hope that they will soon be reunited. She is excited and eager, certain that he will surprise them with a visit at Christmas. As the months and then years go on, however, she is increasingly resigned to the permanence of their separation, and increasingly withdrawn into a melancholy, dreamy, solitary state.

Anaïs included in the diary letters written to her father, and the letters themselves include quotes from her diary. The two are indistinguishable—both poignant efforts to reestablish the lost relationship. But the adolescent diary (1914–20) was not simply a means of communicating with her father; it was a replacement for him. Like Anne, Anaïs imagined the diary as a living person. As she filled each notebook, she bade it farewell, as she would a real person, before greeting the new. What is most essential to her about this imagined presence is that it is steadfast: unlike her father, the diary will not leave her. At twelve, she promised never to abandon it, and demanded the same pledge in return: "Do you promise always to keep the heart that I have given you?" (p. 63). And again, six months later, she wrote that the diary was "doubly dear because it will not desert me." At sixteen, she called it her "best friend on earth, the most faithful, the most sincere" (p. 423).

Like Anne, who can almost convince herself that "Kitty" exists outside of herself, Anaïs fervently wishes to breathe life into the diary. The diary is a letter to her father, it is a replacement for him, and it is the baby she gives him. At sixteen, she wrote:

> If only you had a tongue, my little diary! You know that there was a sculptor who created a statue that came to life, and people who made a snow-child that also came to life! From one moment to the next, I expect a little movement, a smile. I created you. Oh, become somebody! [p. 410]

4 mos.] p. 41). The diary is a friend who, unlike everyone else, does not "misinterpret" Anne's intentions. To put this another way, one might say that the diary does not assert her separateness by seeing things differently than Anne does. There is a fiction, fervently maintained, that the diary is another person; yet this other person, like the mother of infancy, is continuous with the self. It is significant, in this context, that the imaginary confidante in the diaries of adolescent girls is always female (Blos, 1962).

I am reminded of another "illusion" which is invoked at a time of separation, the transitional object of the infant and toddler—the teddy bear or piece of soft blanket that comforts the child in the absence of mother. Winnicott (1953) places these transitional phenomena in an "intermediate area of experiencing" between fantasy and fact, between inner objects and external objects, between subjectivity and objectivity. This is precisely the area occupied by the imagined "other" of the diary. The way in which it is used to "comfort and console" (in Anne's words) is reminiscent of what Winnicott considers the essential quality of the transitional object—its ability to soothe the infant in the absence of the mother. Partaking of mother, it facilitates separation from her. Winnicott proposes that transitional phenomena represent "the early stages of the use of illusion," retained throughout life in the form of creativity.

Anne's invention of "Kitty" also recalls another creation of childhood, the imaginary companion. These are summoned into being by the young child as the repository of standards which are not yet fully internalized

---

The equation of the diary with a baby is explicit in her comment that her imaginary letter to her father was never sent: "I have left it in its cradle and its grave."

The use of the diary as the repository of standards of morality is particularly clear in the diary of Anaïs Nin. She attempts to guide her behavior by precepts she projects onto the diary. Thus, at twelve: "I am full of good resolutions and full of good intentions about keeping them, and each time I would like to break them, my faithful diary and friend will remind me" (p. 53). And similarly, at sixteen: "I can remember things that I haven't done so that I wouldn't have the shame of writing them down; but if I did them, I find them written straight out, spread out here with all the love of truth which is *not* in my character but which *you* have forced me to cultivate" (p. 263, italics in original).

Other adolescent diaries that the reader may find of interest are *A Young Girl's Diary* (1919; New York: Thomas Seltzer, 1921), published with the letter from Freud from which I quoted earlier as preface, and *The Diary of "Helena Morley"* (1893–95; New York: Ecco Press, 1974), the journal of a girl in a small town in Brazil, beautifully translated by the poet Elizabeth Bishop.

(Sperling, 1954; Nagera, 1969). Similarly, Anne invokes "Kitty" to bolster her superego, as if this imagined presence were external to herself, someone upholding standards to which she expects Anne to adhere. After a long, angry passage about her mother, Anne implores "Kitty," "Don't condemn me; remember rather that sometimes I too can reach the bursting point" ([13 yrs., 4 mos.] p. 42). Realizing how many entries have been filled with harsh criticism of her mother, Anne feels a need to justify herself to "Kitty": "My conscience isn't clear as long as I leave you with these accusations, without being able to explain, on looking back, how it happened" ([14 yrs., 6 mos.] p. 114). And again, after a long, excited passage about her increasing intimacy with Peter, Anne concludes, "I must apologize, Kitty, that my style is not up to standard today" ([14 yrs., 9 mos.] p. 163). Here, the disapproval she projects onto "Kitty" for the sexual feeling that she has been describing is displaced onto the writing itself. In adolescence, as inner controls come to feel less reliable, an external presence is again created in fantasy: the fictional "other" of the adolescent diary, like the imaginary companion of the child, embodies values and prohibitions that originally resided in the parents.

I have suggested that the creation of an imagined "other" whom the adolescent brings to life is an effort at restitution for the loss at the heart of the adolescent experience. In this imaginary relationship, the adolescent attempts to recapture and preserve aspects of the earlier relationships with the parents. The imagined "other" of the diary is a presence invoked to meet the specific needs of the adolescent period, but one whose lineage may be traced to earlier illusions created by the child.

The diary of Anne Frank survived her. Four months before the secret annexe would be raided by the Gestapo, she wrote in her diary, "I want to go on living even after my death! And therefore I am grateful to God for giving me this gift, this possibility of developing myself and of writing, of expressing all that is in me" ([14 yrs., 9 mos.] p. 178). Anne's wish has been realized; and we have thereby been left a remarkable documentation of female adolescent development.

Reading the diary, however, we are haunted by the knowledge that Anne was denied the fulfillment of womanhood. She has left us only its promise, poised for completion. How rich that promise was, and how tragic its loss, is evident in what she has given us.

CHAPTER FIVE

Middle Adolescence:
Romeo and Juliet

"**D**eny thy father and refuse thy name," Juliet urges Romeo from her moonlit balcony, and then she continues, "Or if thou wilt not, be but sworn my love / And I'll no longer be a Capulet" (II.ii.34–36). The two had met and fallen in love in an instant earlier that evening when Romeo had come to a masque at the Capulets' home. Now, within their orchard walls, he stands in danger of being killed were her kinsmen to discover him, for as a Montague, Romeo is the Capulets' enemy.

The scene in which these lines are spoken is surely one of the best known and most beloved in literature. Standing on her balcony, unaware at first of Romeo hidden in the darkness below, Juliet goes on to argue, beguilingly, that his family name is no more a part of him than the arbitrary sound signifying the "rose" is a part of the flower. It is a wishful bit of sophistry, as subsequent events prove. But Juliet is entitled to her naiveté: she is just shy of fourteen. Indeed, her age is so important to our understanding of this play that it is reiterated three times in the opening scenes.

Standing on the balcony of her parents' home, urging Romeo to give up the name Montague and offering to abjure her own, Juliet expresses the essential point about falling in love for the first time: the childhood ties to the original family, which are represented here by the family name, must be relinquished. So Juliet asserts, and Romeo agrees, "Call me but love, and I'll be new baptis'd." In this chapter I shall discuss their story as an enduring metaphor for the conflict that inheres in first love. I shall consider the tale of the two warring families of Verona, whose children "unknowingly" fall in love with one another, as a *translation into action* of the central *inner* experience of adolescence. Falling in love with the enemies of their families, Romeo and Juliet have been enacting for centuries the psychological conflict that is at the heart of adolescent love: one's first love is inevitably the enemy of one's family because it is through this love that the power of early ties is diminished.

My discussion will center upon Juliet. She is introduced as a girl, content within her parents' household. In the brief span of the play, as in a time-lapse photograph, we see her become a young woman: her frank welcoming of her awakening sexuality gives the play some of its most superb poetry. Juliet first appears onstage in response to her mother's summons, conveyed by her Nurse, and the words she addresses to her mother are those of an obedient child: "Madam, I am here. What is your will?" Her question is a significant one, marking the starting point for the psychological development I shall trace through the course of the play. At the beginning she asks to know her mother's will. In loving Romeo she comes to know her own will, to disregard and finally to defy that of her parents. Between the first scene and the last, Juliet becomes estranged, one by one, from parental figures—her mother, her father, her Nurse, Friar Lawrence. By the end, she has repudiated the childhood ties to her family and proves herself capable both of courageous independent action and of passionate fidelity in a new love.

The emotional power with which the story continues to engage audiences makes clear its resonance with psychological realities not limited by the particulars of the time and place in which it was written. Indeed, the tale of Romeo and Juliet had its origins in folklore and was well known before Shakespeare adapted it to the stage. From its roots in folklore, the story had been developed in the fifteenth and sixteenth centuries by a series of European writers of *novelle*; it achieved considerable popularity in England after it was translated into English in 1562 by Arthur Brooke. Brooke's long poem, "The Tragicall Historye of Romeus and Juliet," was the primary source for the play, perhaps the only source. Verbal similarities at many points prove that Shakespeare drew closely on Brooke's poem; but he modified it as well, in ways that matter to my concerns here.

To begin, he altered Juliet's age. In Brooke's poem she is sixteen; in another possible source (William Painter's *Palace of Pleasure,* 1567) she is eighteen. Shakespeare's Juliet is just under fourteen, and much is made of her youthfulness in the opening scenes. Her Nurse even gives us Juliet's birthday precisely: "Come Lammas Eve at night shall she be fourteen." The date itself is of interest. In the early English church, Lammas, the first day of August, was traditionally a harvest festival for the first ripe corn, from which loaves were made and consecrated. Thus not only Juliet's tender age but the very date of her birth has associations of early ripening.

Events which, in Brooke's poem, extend over months, are here quickened in pace. In Brooke's poem, Romeo and Juliet first meet at the Capulet's masked ball at Christmastime. Romeo then passes back and forth under her balcony for a week or two before they speak to one another; it is the day after Easter—three months after their marriage—when Romeo is accosted by Tybalt and kills him. Shakespeare compresses these events into just four days, giving the play an atmosphere of urgency and intensity that corresponds to the inner state of the young lovers. But most importantly, Shakespeare draws us into a profoundly sympathetic relation with Romeo and Juliet, unlike Brooke, who censures them. In the prologue to his poem, Brooke declares that he is setting out to show:

> A coople of unfortunate lovers, thralling themselves to unhonest desire, neglecting the authoritie and advise of parents and frendes . . . attemptyng all adventures of peryll, for thattaynyng of their wished lust . . . abusyng the honorable name of lawefull marriage, the cloke the shame of stolne contractes, finallye, by all means of unhonest lyfe, hastyng to most unhappye deathe.

In contrast, what Shakespeare gives us is the *subjective experience* of adolescent passion. It is conveyed not only in the poetry in which Romeo and Juliet directly speak their love—the sonnet they share upon meeting, Juliet's epithalamium anticipating their wedding night, the aubade when they must part. Not only the poetry, but the story itself, the structure of the play, the changing ways in which language is used, the characterization of those surrounding the lovers—all mirror the inner experience of adolescence.

When the play begins, Romeo is already in love, not with Juliet but with a young woman named Rosaline. When he first comes onstage, self-absorbed and self-pitying, he is made to seem foolish. He proclaims his love in a series of conceits and oxymora that were highly conventional within the Petrarchan tradition and would have been heard as clichés by the Elizabethan audience:

> Why then, O brawling love, O loving hate,
> O anything of nothing first create!

> O heavy lightness, serious vanity,
> Misshapen chaos of well-seeming forms!
> Feather of lead, bright smoke, cold fire, sick health,
> Still-waking sleep that is not what it is!
> This love feel I that feel no love in this.
> Dost thou not laugh?
>
> [I.i.174–81]

Shakespeare is here smiling at Romeo—as well as at a literary tradition—and inviting us to do the same. Indeed, within the play Romeo is affectionately mocked by his friends Benvolio and Mercutio, and even by the mild Friar Lawrence, who, when Romeo declares his love for Juliet, pretends still to see on Romeo's face traces of the tears shed for Rosaline. This shadowy figure, of whom we hear much in the early part of the play, never appears onstage. She must remain a creature of the audience's imagination, much as she is of Romeo's. Rather, what we are shown is the response of those around him to Romeo's state of mind. Pining for Rosaline, Romeo is the adolescent lover as he appears to others. The love of Romeo and Juliet is adolescent love as it *feels*.

By compressing the action to just four days, Shakespeare has charged the play with feverish intensity. Within its brief span, life is lived at those heights of feeling at which the experience of time is altered. Juliet is always at odds with time, imploring it to go faster or slower. Waiting for the Nurse to bring word from Romeo, she feels the passage of time to be unendurably slow: "Love's heralds should be thoughts / Which ten times faster glides than the sun's beams." Anticipating her wedding night, she implores day to end and night to come "immediately." And after their wedding night, when Romeo must leave, Juliet desperately tries to believe that it was the nightingale they heard and not the lark. When she must admit, finally, that it is indeed dawn, she urges Romeo to send word often, "For in a minute there are many days." Adults in the play have a different experience of time; they counsel moderation in feeling. Lady Capulet, believing Juliet to be weeping for the death of her cousin, instructs her that grief should be contained within proper limits. Similarly, Friar Lawrence, sensing danger in the intensity of their youthful passion, cautions Romeo and Juliet,

> Therefore love moderately; long love doth so.
> Too swift arrives as tardy as too slow.
>
> [II.vi.14–15]

In a play that has attuned our ears to paradox and oxymoron on the subject of love, his advice to "love moderately" sounds a contradiction in terms.

The play is peopled by characters who justify the conviction of adolescent lovers that their experience is unprecedented and unique—who "jest at scars that never felt a wound," as Romeo says of Mercutio, who "speak of that thou dost not feel," as he says to Friar Lawrence. The parental figures of the play mirror the representation of parents in adolescent perception and fantasy. The Nurse, who at first seems a fond maternal presence, will finally show herself to be self-interested, envious, even cruel to Juliet, as I shall elaborate. Similarly, the father's loving protectiveness toward his daughter will become tyrannical control, an arbitrary and capricious exercise of power over her.

Juliet's love for Romeo is counterposed to another possible alliance, that with Paris. This advantageous match, the one favored by Juliet's parents, urged and finally forced by them, is presented as such a match would appear to an adolescent—dreary and empty of everything but form. Even the praise of Paris is set in contexts that alienate rather than engage our sympathies. When Lady Capulet compares him, in a series of rhymed couplets, to a book, she intends the conceit to flatter; but in this drama of intense passion, being compared to a book is faint praise indeed.[1] And when events have begun rushing toward disaster, and the Nurse urges Juliet now to forget Romeo and marry Paris ("Oh, he's a lovely gentleman. / Romeo's a dishclout to him"), she reveals more tellingly her own lack of fidelity than Paris's virtues. He is damned by such praise.

The role of Paris in the play is another of Shakespeare's innovations: it is greatly enlarged from what it had been in Brooke's poem. Shakespeare introduces him early, in the second scene of the play, when he enters as Romeo exits. Until the final scene in the tomb, when he challenges Romeo and is killed by him, Paris remains a constant presence whose conventional suit, that which the parents approve, is contrasted

---

1. Mercutio insults Tybalt by saying that he duels "by the book," and Juliet gently mocks Romeo when she accuses him of kissing "by the book." It is only when she is angry at Romeo, having just learned that he has killed her cousin, that she echoes her mother's conceit: "Was ever book containing such vile matter / So fairly bound?" And when the lovers can hardly bear to part, Romeo observes, "Love goes toward love as schoolboys from their books, / But love from love, toward school with heavy looks" (II.ii.156–57). Books are to be endured; passion lies elsewhere.

with the secret passion of Romeo and Juliet. The language spoken by the two young men is used to control and direct our sympathies. Paris is given language that is stiff and formal, setting him at a distance. When Juliet is found seemingly dead, his speech:

> Beguil'd, divorced, wronged, spited, slain.
> Most detestable Death, by thee beguil'd,
> By cruel, cruel thee quite overthrown.
> Oh love! Oh life! Not life, but love in death!

is indistinguishable in style from that of her father, which continues directly from it and mirrors its structure precisely:

> Despis'd, distressed, hated, martyr'd, kill'd.
> Uncomfortable time, why cam'st thou now
> To murder, murder our solemnity?
> O child, O child! My soul and not my child,
> Dead art thou.
>
> [IV.v. 55–63]

Compare with these speeches Romeo's terse and powerful response on being told that Juliet is dead: "Is it e'en so? Then I defy you stars!"

By the end, Romeo has ceased to be the foolish adolescent in love with the stock phrases of love. What Paris feels can still be expressed through received verbal and rhetorical convention, but this is no longer adequate for Romeo. The maturation of both hero and heroine requires language that becomes more spontaneous and more particularly their own. It is not only their actions, but their use of language itself that marks their emergence as individuals and their estrangement from the world of their parents.

The youthfulness of Romeo and Juliet at the beginning of the play is underscored in many ways. Before either of them appears on stage, we see them through the eyes of their parents. Our first such view is of Romeo. His parents express concern that he has become withdrawn of late, moody and secretive, and has rebuffed his father's attempts to learn the cause of his dark humor. Worried, and wishing to know more, they must turn to their son's friend Benvolio, who, they know, will have greater access to his confidence than they themselves. Before leaving the two alone to talk, the parents poignantly express the belief that, as with a young child, they still have the power to "make it better": "Could we but learn from whence his sorrows grow / We would as willingly give cure as know."

Romeo's age is not stated, but his phase of development is altogether recognizable. His adolescence has begun. He has withdrawn from his parents and is more intimate now with his friends—friends of his own sex and his own age. Such friendships, as I have said, are the hallmark of the early adolescent phase, preceding the turn toward the opposite sex that usually characterizes middle adolescence. Romeo's exchanges with Benvolio and Mercutio, their banter, their ease in one another's presence, their familiar ways of playing off one another's jokes all convince us that there is a history to their friendship. Now, Romeo's infatuation with Rosaline is beginning to set him apart from his male friends as well. Pining for Rosaline, he wanders alone before dawn, avoiding their company and evading their questions.[2] But Rosaline is unmoved by his pursuit. "She hath forsworn to love," Romeo laments to his friend:

> she'll not be hit
> With Cupid's arrow, she hath Dian's wit,
> And in strong proof of chastity well arm'd
> From love's weak childish bow she lives uncharm'd.
>
> [I.i.206–09]

Thus, in his first venture outside the familiarity and safety of the male world of friendship, Romeo makes a choice that is often characteristic of this transitional point: he chooses a woman who is safely unavailable. He may dote on her, he may pine for her, but she remains a solitary fantasy. There is some pleasant melancholy to be savored, but no danger in loving the chaste Rosaline. Romeo's estrangement from his friends will deepen when he turns from a woman who is unavailable to one who reciprocates his passion.[3]

2. Dickey (1957) discusses the melancholy lover in the writings of sixteenth-century physicians and in literary tradition.

3. The male world of Romeo, Benvolio, and Mercutio shares important features with the male world of the feud, the background against which the story of the lovers is set. In the opening scene of the play, Sampson and Gregory, servants of the Capulets, appear onstage punning broadly, admiring their own wit, itching for a fight, and goading one another on. The wordplay the servants so relish—boasting of "standing" and "thrusting," grinning about drawing their "tools" and having their "naked weapons" out—has a single theme, and the banter of the young nobles is filled with the same innuendo, the same double entendre. Mercutio puns as broadly in blank verse as the

But at the outset Juliet is still a child, content within her father's household. Before she appears onstage she, too, is pictured through the eyes of a parent. Capulet, speaking with her suitor, Paris, is trying to put off the question of marriage, emphasizing his daughter's inexperience of life:[4]

> My child is yet a stranger in the world,
> She hath not seen the change of fourteen years.
> Let two more summers wither in their pride
> Ere we may think her ripe to be a bride.
>
> [I.ii.8–11]

When we meet Juliet directly, she is ensconsed in the bosom of her family, in conversation with two maternal figures—her mother and her Nurse. Her father told us her age in the previous scene, and now Lady Capulet reminds us of it again. But to say of Juliet, as her mother does, simply that "she's not fourteen" is not exact enough for the Nurse, to whom everything about Juliet matters greatly. She adds that she can tell Juliet's age "unto an hour": "Come Lammas Eve at night shall she be fourteen." This is the third time we are told Juliet's age, and her birthday itself, as I have indicated, has associations of early ripening. It quickly

---

servants had done in prose about "raising him up" and "letting it there stand." It is all one joke.

It is noteworthy that no woman expresses the remotest interest in the feud. When the two patriarchs, Montague and Capulet, try to join in the fighting, they are restrained from doing so by their wives. And after the brawl, speaking with Benvolio, Lady Montague does not say she wishes that Romeo had been there to defend the family honor. On the contrary, she immediately expresses relief that he was not involved. Women are not engaged by the feud; it is something to keep their husbands and sons out of. (See Kahn's [1977] discussion of the social context of the feud.)

The ethos of the feud is one that excludes women and makes no sense to them. Its quality of childish braggadocio is characteristic of the early phase of male adolescence when boys take refuge in the company of other boys. They may ignore girls or deride them, but most importantly they stay away from them. In risqué jokes there is a relentless celebration of that which the female does not have, and which must be protected from her imagined power.

4. We are evidently meant to think of Juliet as young for marriage. Stone (1977) concludes from contemporary records that daughters of the upper landed classes in England married, on the average, at about twenty in the late sixteenth century. Laslett (1971), on the basis of marriage licenses issued in Canterbury, finds that among the gentry in the early to mid-seventeenth century, the average age of marriage for a woman was about twenty-one.

becomes clear that the Nurse dotes on the girl. After she has been asked, twice, to hold her peace, still she cannot refrain from adding that Juliet was the prettiest baby she ever nursed. When finally Lady Capulet broaches her subject and Juliet speaks her few words of reply, this is sufficient cue to bring forth still another burst of praise from the Nurse. Juliet says of marriage simply, "It is an honour that I dream not of," but her Nurse cannot help admiring: "An honour. Were not I thine only nurse / I would say thou hadst suck'd wisdom from thy teat" (I.iii.67–68).

Lady Capulet has summoned Juliet to urge that she accept the suit of Paris. The Nurse adds her own encouragement for the match, but not without first reminiscing—at length—about Juliet's childhood. Her affectionate reminiscence has been much admired and commented upon as a means of characterizing the Nurse herself. Coleridge, for example, compared her presentation here to a portrait "in which every hair was so exquisitely painted that it would bear the test of a microscope." He saw in her rambling, anecdotal speech "all the garrulity of age," strengthened by the prerogative of a long-trusted servant. In her piling on of incident—to comic effect—commentators have seen the working of an uncultivated mind, which links events solely by their coincidence in time, but goes off on a tangent as soon as some new idea enters her head.

I would like to suggest another way of looking at the Nurse's speech. This woman had been Juliet's wet nurse as well as her governess. And it is noteworthy, therefore, that the memory she evokes in her reminiscence is *not* that of the infant, blissfully asleep at the breast. Such a memory would equally have served to establish her status as trusted servant and her fondness for the girl she nursed and raised. But significantly, the memory she now evokes, so vividly, is that of the toddler being *weaned* from the breast. In this, our introduction to Juliet, the developmental context established by the Nurse's reminiscence is that of the child's first separation from the mothering figure. The day Juliet was weaned is a day the Nurse recalls with absolute clarity:

'Tis since the earthquake now eleven years,
And she was wean'd—I never shall forget it—
Of all the days of the year upon that day.
For I had then laid wormwood to my dug,
Sitting in the sun under the dovehouse wall.
My lord and you were then at Mantua—

Nay I do bear a brain. But as I said,
When it did taste the wormwood on the nipple
Of my dug and felt it bitter, pretty fool,
To see it tetchy and fall out with the dug.
Shake! quoth the dovehouse. 'Twas no need, I trow,
To bid me trudge.
And since that time it is eleven years.
For then she could stand high-lone, nay, by th'rood,
She could have run and waddled all about;
For even the day before she broke her brow,
And then my husband—God be with his soul,
A was a merry man—took up the child,
"Yea," quoth he, "dost thou fall upon thy face?
Thou wilt fall backward when thou hast more wit,
Wilt thou not, Jule?" And by my holidame,
The pretty wretch left crying and said "Ay."

[I.iii.23–44]

With Juliet at the threshold of adolescence, the Nurse reaches back in memory specifically to those achievements which signal the beginning autonomy of the young child—the time when she was first able to stand alone and walk by herself, the day that she was weaned. The Nurse evokes the period with an immediacy of detail: she allows us, with her, to see the child's first steps, punctuated by frequent falling, to hear the first words, not fully understood, that mesh with adult speech in random ways that are inadvertently meaningful and humorous. Just the day before she was weaned, little Juliet had stumbled and fallen, getting a bump on her forehead which made her cry bitterly. Now, eleven years later, the Nurse cannot help but laugh when she recalls her husband's joke and the child's unknowing response:

"Yea," quoth my husband, "fall'st upon thy face?
Thou wilt fall backward when thou comest to age,
Wilt thou not, Jule?" It stinted, and said "Ay."

[I.iii.55–57]

The Nurse is so fond of the joke that after telling it once, she tells it three more times. Repeated thus, it becomes an important part of the background for what is to follow. In response to the falling of the toddler, her husband had anticipated Juliet's coming of age. Like the reminiscence in which it is embedded, his bawdy joke intuits a connection between the two periods of life—the earlier period of separation and that which is now beginning.[5]

When we first meet Juliet, however, her adolescence has not yet begun. The starting point for her development, I have suggested, is marked by the first words she addresses to her mother: "Madam, I am here, what is your will?" Lady Capulet has summoned her to discuss the subject of marriage. Juliet is urged to consider Paris both by her mother and by her Nurse, who chimes in her own—very different—view of the advantages of the match. Juliet agrees to pay special attention to the young man, who has been invited to the Capulets' masque. At the close of the scene she underscores once again her childlike obedience to the wishes of her parents:

> I'll look to like, if looking liking move,
> But no more deep will I endart mine eye
> Than your consent gives strength to make it fly.
>
> [I.iii.97–99]

Juliet is introduced in colloquy with two maternal figures, and the two women are strongly contrasted. Lady Capulet appears tense and agitated as she first dismisses the Nurse, then calls her back:

> This is the matter. Nurse, give leave awhile,
> We must talk in secret. Nurse, come back again,
> I have remember'd me, thou's hear our counsel.
>
> [I.iii.7–9]

Once the Nurse returns, it is she whom Lady Capulet addresses, rather than Juliet: "Thou knowest my daugher's of a pretty age." The Nurse then proceeds to her reminiscence, in the course of which she mentions her wish that she may live to see Juliet married. Lady Capulet uses this as the means, finally, to broach her subject: "Marry, that marry is the very theme / I came to talk of." Her play on words and the stilted, constrained tone of her speech contrasts with the spontaneity and expansiveness of the Nurse's discourse. The child was "Jule" to the Nurse's late husband, but Lady Capulet uses no terms of endearment, no nick-

---

5. The Nurse would seem to be anticipating, by some four centuries, Blos's (1967) conception of adolescence as "the second individuation process," parallel to that of the early years.

names, makes no reference to a shared past. There is a stiff formality to Lady Capulet's speech, while the Nurse's recollections have the quality of sensory impressions: on that day eleven years ago when she applied wormwood to her nipple in order to wean Juliet, she was sitting in the sun under the dovehouse wall. In her mind's eye, she not only sees Juliet recoil, she imagines the child's experience in tasting the wormwood and finding it bitter. Her description of the tremor of the dovehouse caused by the earthquake—"Shake, quoth the dovehouse"—is animistic and picturesque.

Through her reminiscence, the Nurse is immediately established as an appealing character. Her recollections of the past—in abundant detail—indicate the importance Juliet has had for her, taking the place, perhaps, of her own child. She alludes to her own losses—the daughter, Susan, who would have been the same age as Juliet (it is the only time she is mentioned, but her being given a name sharpens the implied loss), and her husband, "a merry man," whose joke still makes her laugh eleven years later. We, and Juliet, will come to see the Nurse differently, but it is important, in this play about adolescence, that at the outset the Nurse appears to be a warm and sympathetic figure. This was the woman with whom Juliet shared her childhood, who nursed her and weaned her, who saw her first tottering steps, who heard her first words. Indeed, on the day the Nurse fondly recalls, when Juliet was weaned, her parents were away in Mantua.

The presence of the Nurse offers the modern audience a glimpse into the practice of wet-nursing, the usual urban and upper-class practice during the Renaissance. A woman of Lady Capulet's social position would not have been expected to nurse her child. It is a piece of history, but it also has a metaphoric resonance which is not limited to its period. The presence of two maternal figures corresponds to a "split" that exists in the very young child's mental representation of the mother. In infancy, disparate experiences of mother have not yet fused into a single whole: it represents a profound psychic achievement when "good mother" and "bad mother" become one mother, ambivalently regarded, but nonetheless constant in her inner representation.[6] The experience of "two mothers" is often defensively revived in adolescence, when the sexuality which must now be denied in the mother is vividly perceived in (or projected

6. See Lustman (1977) for a critical review of the concept of splitting in the psychoanalytic literature.

onto) another woman. The contrast between Lady Capulet and the Nurse corresponds to such a split. The exuberant bawdiness of the Nurse is conveyed in her very first words onstage. In response to Lady Capulet's impatient summoning of her daughter, the Nurse goes off to call her again: "Now by my maidenhead at twelve years old, / I bade her come." The joke is that she could not safely swear by her maidenhead at thirteen.

The Nurse is a lusty, full-blooded woman, contrasted with the thin-blooded, thin-lipped Lady Capulet. The Nurse is fondly garrulous, but her mother speaks tersely to Juliet: "Thus then in brief: / The valiant Paris seeks you for his love." And after praising Paris, she brusquely asks, "Speak briefly, can you like of Paris' love?" The difference between these two maternal figures is most succinctly conveyed in their different ways of construing how Juliet would gain by marrying Paris. Lady Capulet compares him, in a succession of rhymed couplets, to a book:

> Read o'er the volume of young Paris' face
> And find delight writ there with beauty's pen.
> Examine every married lineament
> And see how one another lends content;
> And what obscur'd in this fair volume lies,
> Find written in the margent of his eyes.
> This precious book of love, this unbound lover,
> To beautify him only lacks a cover.
> The fish lives in the sea; and 'tis much pride
> For fair without the fair within to hide.
> That book in many's eyes doth share the glory
> That in gold clasps locks in the golden story.

The conceit is a conventional one, and each new turn of the metaphor fits exactly its allotted couplet. Lady Capulet concludes her recommendation,

> So shall you share all that he doth possess,
> By having him, making yourself no less.

> [I.iii.81–94]

And the Nurse chimes in, "No less, nay bigger. Women grow by men." Lady Capulet is thinking of wealth; the Nurse is thinking of pregnancy. And in the final line of the scene, after Lady Capulet has commended Paris by comparing him to a book, the Nurse urges her own view of the advantages of marriage: "Go girl, seek happy nights to happy days." Her exuberant anticipation of "happy nights" in the marriage bed makes clear that the Nurse is a woman for whom the body and its pleasures have been central. She has hardly bustled onstage before alluding to having, now, only four teeth remaining; as the play proceeds, we will see more fully her response to the inexorable failing of her body—and its effect on her relation with the young Juliet.

In the Nurse and in her father, Juliet has two parental figures who are acutely aware of their advancing age. It is of crucial importance, in this play about adolescents, that from the beginning the youthfulness of the lovers is set against the aging of the parental generation. In the opening scene of the brawl in the streets, Capulet comes onstage calling for his long sword, only to have his wife mockingly respond, "A crutch, a crutch! Why call you for a sword?" In the scene that follows, there is another immediate reference to his age and to the stilling of passions. Speaking with Paris about the truce imposed on both sides, Capulet says of himself and the other patriarch, Montague, "Tis not hard I think / For men as old as we to keep the peace."

Capulet's own awareness that he is growing old, however, is most fully developed in the scene of the masque: it is the background against which the meeting of Romeo and Juliet is set. Capulet greets his guests:

> Welcome, gentlemen. I have seen the day
> That I have worn a visor and could tell
> A whispering tale in a fair lady's ear,
> Such as would please. 'Tis gone, 'tis gone, 'tis gone,
> You are welcome, gentlemen: come, musicians, play.
> A hall, a hall, give room! And foot it girls!
>
> [I.v.21–26]

Capulet's reference to his ability, in years past, to please the ladies, and his wistful acknowledgment, repeated three times, that this ability is now gone, is juxtaposed with his welcoming remarks. As pater familias and host, he urges the musicians to play—for a dance at which he can now be only a spectator.

Indeed, he turns to a relative, observing that "you and I are past our dancing days," and engages him in conversation about when they themselves were last in a masque. The man replies that it is thirty years, and Capulet protests—it cannot be that long, surely it is only twenty-five years. But his kinsman is quite clear: it was a wedding when last they masqued, and the child of this marriage is now thirty. Still, Capulet is disbelieving. Surely it was just two years ago that the son was "but a ward" i.e., a minor, under twenty-one. The gist of their conversation is clear: our children grow up faster than we realize, and thereby remind us that we ourselves are correspondingly aged.

This heavily underscored presentation of Capulet's aging constitutes the background for Romeo's first sight of Juliet. Romeo's passionate response to her beauty is directly juxtaposed with the father's wistful incredulity about how quickly life is passing:

> *Cap.* Nay sit, nay sit, good cousin Capulet
> For you and I are past our dancing days.
> How long is't now since last yourself and I
> Were in a masque?
> *Cousin Cap.*   By'r Lady, thirty years.
> *Cap.* What, man, 'tis not so much, 'tis not so much.
> 'Tis since the nuptial of Lucentio,
> Come Pentecost as quickly as it will,
> Some five and twenty years: and then we masqu'd.
> *Cousin Cap.* 'Tis more, 'tis more, his son is elder, sir:
> His son is thirty.
> *Cap.*   Will you tell me that?
> His son was but a ward two years ago.

Then follows immediately:

> *Romeo.* What lady's that which doth enrich the hand
> Of yonder knight?
> *Ser.*   I know not, sir.
> *Romeo.* O, she doth teach the torches to burn bright.
> It seems she hangs upon the cheek of night
> As a rich jewel in an Ethiop's ear—
> Beauty too rich for use, for earth too dear.
>
> [I.v.30–46]

Romeo's first words to Juliet begin a sonnet which leads to their first kiss:

> *Romeo.* If I profane with my unworthiest hand
> This holy shrine, the gentle sin is this:
> My lips, two blushing pilgrims, ready stand
> To smooth that rough touch with a tender kiss.

> *Juliet.* Good pilgrim, you do wrong your hand too much,
>   Which mannerly devotion shows in this;
>   For saints have hands that pilgrims' hands do touch,
>   And palm to palm is holy palmers' kiss.
> *Romeo.* Have not saints lips, and holy palmers too?
> *Juliet.* Ay, pilgrim, lips that they must use in prayer.
> *Romeo.* O then, dear saint, let lips do what hands do:
>   They pray: grant thou, lest faith turn to despair.
> *Juliet.* Saints do not move, though grant for prayer's sake.
> *Romeo.* Then move not, while my prayer's effect I take.
>   [*He kisses her.*]
>   [I.v.92–105]

Unlike Romeo's earlier literary efforts, whose subject was the unresponsive Rosaline, this sonnet is taken up and shared by Juliet. Their touch, and then their kiss, are indeed, as Romeo observes, "trespass sweetly urg'd" by her. And after their first kiss, Juliet gently and playfully prompts him to kiss her again, by saying that now her own lips have the sin they took from his—which he, of course, immediately offers to take back.

With these lines, they have begun another sonnet (this time kissing after only the first quatrain) when the Nurse interrupts: "Madam, your mother craves a word with you." This interruption signals the dialectic that will continue throughout the play in the tension between Juliet's movement toward Romeo and her parents' attempts to pull her back. The progress of their love is set against the background of—and is always in conflict with—Juliet's ties to her family.

In this, her first encounter with Romeo, we begin to see those qualities which will become more and more distinctively Juliet's: her candor, humor, playfulness—and her welcoming of her awakening sexuality. In the earlier scene, when Juliet had appeared in response to the Nurse's call, we were introduced to an obedient child, submissive to the wishes of her parents. Now, having met Romeo and kissed him, having fallen in love, Juliet begins to use guile in relation to her Nurse. As the guests leave, Juliet asks the Nurse their names, first indicating two others before pointing out the one who in fact inspires her question. Upon learning Romeo's name, she expresses surprise and dismay:

> My only love sprung from my only hate.
> Too early seen unknown, and known too late.

> Prodigious birth of love it is to me
> That I must love a loathed enemy.

[I.v.137–40]

The Nurse asks what she is talking about and Juliet lies, saying off-handedly that it was just "a rhyme I learn'd even now / Of one I danc'd withal."

Romeo has a similar response when he is told Juliet's name: "Is she a Capulet? / O dear account. My life is my foe's debt." He claims surprise on learning that Juliet is a Capulet, but so was Rosaline, who is Capulet's niece—and he has come, after all, to a masque at the Capulets' home. In loving first Rosaline, then Juliet, Romeo feels the choice to have been unwitting, but he expressly chooses those who would estrange him from the Montagues.

I have suggested that their situation may be considered a metaphor for what is actually an *internal* conflict in adolescence: that one's first love is inevitably the enemy of one's family, because it is through this love that the strength of the ties to the original family is weakened. This is explicitly the subject of their discourse in the scene in which Romeo and Juliet declare their love. Juliet steps out from her father's house onto her balcony and begins the soliloquy from which I quoted at the beginning of the chapter:

> O Romeo, Romeo, wherefore art thou Romeo?
> Deny thy father and refuse thy name.
> Or if thou wilt not, be but sworn my love
> And I'll no longer be a Capulet.

[II.ii.33–36]

"Deny thy father": the substance of her meditation is that in loving one another she and Romeo must renounce the ties to their parents that their family names represent. She goes on, "Tis but thy name that is my enemy: / Thou art thyself, though not a Montague," as if his "self" were separate from his being a Montague. Her well-known speech beginning, "What's in a name?" continues this effort to deny the strength of the ties to the family. She argues that Romeo's being a Montague is "no part" of him, but is extrinsic and arbitrary, like the sound "rose" that signifies the flower.

> What's Montague? It is nor hand nor foot
> Nor arm nor face nor any other part

Belonging to a man. O be some other name.
What's in a name? That which we call a rose
By any other word would smell as sweet;
So Romeo would, were he not Romeo call'd,
Retain that dear perfection which he owes
Without that title. Romeo, doff thy name,
And for thy name, which is no part of thee,
Take all myself.

[II.ii.40–49]

At this point, Romeo steps from the shadows, completing her line. He shares her wishful belief that the ties to the original family may be lightly cast off:

I take thee at thy word.
Call me but love, and I'll be new baptis'd:
Henceforth I never will be Romeo.

[II.ii.49–51]

The imagery they use throughout this scene suggests that their love for one another not only constitutes a casting off of familial ties, but that it is a *replacement* for these ties.

Hidden in the orchard, Romeo had overheard Juliet's confession of love before she was aware of his presence. Once he steps from the darkness, she says that were it not for the mask of night covering her face, she would blush for what he has overheard. She refers ironically to the conventions that usually govern the behavior of lovers:

Fain would I dwell on form; fain, fain deny
What I have spoke. But farewell, compliment.
Dost thou love me? I know thou wilt say "Ay,"
And I will take thy word. Yet, if thou swear'st,
Thou mayst prove false. At lovers' perjuries,
They say, Jove laughs. O gentle Romeo,
If thou dost love, pronounce it faithfully.
Or, if thou think'st I am too quickly won,
I'll frown and be perverse and say thee nay,
So thou wilt woo; but else, not for the world.
In truth, fair Montague, I am too fond,
And therefore thou mayst think my haviour light,

> But trust me, gentleman, I'll prove more true
> Than those that have more cunning to be strange.
>
> [II.ii.88–101]

"Fain would I dwell on form," she says, alluding to the usual rituals of courtship. But Juliet is incapable of dwelling on form. Her freshness, directness, and spontaneity—her mischievous humor—burst through the constraints of form. The simplicity of Juliet's utterance contrasts with the extravagance and artificiality of Romeo's speech. Shaped by feeling, Juliet's sentences end mid-line; Romeo's conform to metric demands. Romeo looks to the heavens for his metaphors, but Juliet draws on the proximal senses. She smells the rose; her ears "drink the words" of his "tongue's uttering." Romeo compares Juliet to the sun, to the stars, to an angel bestriding the clouds; she is a "winged messenger of heaven" appearing "unto the white-upturned wondering eyes / Of mortals that fall back to gaze." He would venture after her were she "as far / As that vast shore wash'd with the farthest sea." Romeo's imagery places her off at a distance; Juliet's language brings him close. What belongs to a rose is its sweet smell; what belongs to a man is his body.

Juliet's concern for Romeo's safety in the Capulet orchard prompts her to ask questions that are practical and down-to-earth. To her worried questions, he replies with flights of rhetoric:

> *Juliet.* How cam'st thou hither, tell me, and wherefore?
>   The orchard walls are high and hard to climb,
>   And the place death, considering who thou art,
>   If any of my kinsmen find thee here.
> *Romeo.* With love's light wings did I o'erperch these walls,
>   For stony limits cannot hold love out,
>   And what love can do, that dares love attempt:
>   Therefore thy kinsmen are no stop to me.
>
> [II.ii.62–69]

When Juliet expresses alarm about his very survival, Romeo's answer displays a foolish bravado—and a fondness for romantic cliché:

> Alack, there lies more peril in thine eye
> Than twenty of their swords.

Juliet shows gentle humor at the expense of Romeo's romanticizing. When he begins his declaration of love,

Lady, by yonder blessed moon I vow,
That tips with silver all these fruit-tree tops—

she interrupts him mid-conceit to object to his swearing by the incon-
stant moon, "lest that thy love prove likewise variable." When he begins
afresh, "If my heart's dear love—" she again interrupts him: "Well, do
not swear." Romeo is always in deadly earnest; Juliet has a twinkle in
her eye.

Having abjured the conventions of courtship, Juliet herself asks Romeo
to declare his love, and it is she who initiates talk of marriage. She is
the more active and clear-headed of the two; Romeo retains, still, the
aspect of the lovesick boy, enamored of love's literary tradition. Even as
he casts about for some metaphor in which to express his love, Juliet
has a foreboding of its ultimate outcome:

Although I joy in thee,
I have no joy of this contract tonight:
It is too rash, to unadvis'd, too sudden,
Too like the lightning, which doth cease to be
Ere one can say 'It lightens'.

Again their conversation is interrupted by the Nurse, who calls to
Juliet from within her father's house. Juliet goes inside, then returns to
propose marriage. She has barely finished when again the Nurse calls to
her. Juliet must interrupt herself—twice—to call back, but still she
manages not to lose the thread of her dialogue with Romeo:

Juliet. Three words, dear Romeo, and good night indeed.
If that thy bent of love be honourable,
Thy purpose marriage, send me word tomorrow
By one that I'll procure to come to thee,
Where and what time thou wilt perform the rite,
And all my fortunes at thy foot I'll lay,
And follow thee my lord throughout the world.
Nurse. [*Within.*] Madam.
Juliet. I come, anon—But if thou meanest not well
I do beseech thee—
Nurse. [*Within.*]   Madam.

Juliet.   By and by I come—
    To cease thy strife and leave me to my grief.
    Tomorrow will I send.

[II.ii.142–53]

When next we see Juliet, it is noon of the following day. The Nurse
set out at nine, promising to return in half an hour with word from
Romeo of when and where the marriage will take place, and still she
has not come. Juliet can hardly bear the waiting:

O, she is lame. Love's heralds should be thoughts
Which ten times faster glides than the sun's beams
Driving back shadows over lowering hills.
Therefore do nimble-pinion'd doves draw Love,
And therefore hath the wind-swift Cupid wings.
Now is the sun upon the highmost hill
Of this day's journey, and from nine till twelve
Is three long hours, yet she is not come.
Had she affections and warm youthful blood
She would be as swift in motion as a ball:
My words would bandy her to my sweet love,
And his to me.

[II.v.4–15]

When finally the Nurse appears, Juliet's impatience agitates the rhythm
of her language: "O God she comes. O honey Nurse, what news? / Hast
thou met with him?" The Nurse responds irrelevantly by complaining of
fatigue, of the aching of her bones. Juliet replies drily, "I would thou
hadst my bones and I thy news," then presses her again to speak. The
Nurse continues to withhold the news, complaining now of being out of
breath, then rebuking Juliet for being impatient. Juliet's response is
commonsensical and clear-headed:

How art thou out of breath when thou hast breath
To say to me that thou art out of breath?
The excuse that thou dost make in this delay
Is longer than the tale thou dost excuse.
Is thy news good or bad? Answer to that,

Say either, and I'll stay the circumstance.
Let me be satisfied: is't good or bad?

[II.v.31–37]

Still, the Nurse makes her wait longer by complaining further—now about the aching of her head, now about the aching of her back. Juliet becomes exasperated but conducts herself as a well brought-up young lady, telling the Nurse she is sorry that she is not well and obediently bringing a poultice for her aching bones. Twice, when the Nurse seems finally on the point of telling the girl what she is bursting to know, she interrupts herself with tangential questions: Has Juliet dined at home? Where is her mother? In the face of considerable provocation, Juliet remains polite and even keeps her sense of humor:

> *Nurse.* Your love says like an honest gentleman,
>   And a courteous, and a kind, and a handsome,
>   And I warrant a virtuous—Where is your mother?
> *Juliet.* Where is my mother? Why, she is within.
>   Where should she be? How oddly thou repliest.
>   "Your love says, like an honest gentleman,
>   " 'Where is your mother?' "

[II.v.56–62]

In all, the Nurse makes Juliet wait for seventy lines before she reveals the arrangements for her marriage.

We already know that the Nurse is a maddening temporizer, a woman incapable of speaking briefly. In her reminiscence about Juliet's childhood, she was ramblingly anecdotal in a way that there was humorous and appealing. But now there is another aspect to what had earlier seemed benign. The Nurse's withholding of essential information for which Juliet has already waited three hours is teasing that verges on cruelty. In the earlier scene, her reminiscence about the past made it clear that she had doted on the young Jule and conveyed, movingly, a sense of their shared past. We may ask, then, what underlies the marked change in her behavior toward Juliet now. An answer is suggested by the tactic she uses to delay. While complaining at length about the failing of her own body, the Nurse reveals that she is acutely aware of the beauty of Romeo's youthful body. In the midst of her complaints, she indicates that she has cast a carefully appraising eye over it. Still withholding what Juliet wants to know, the Nurse observes, lapsing into prose,

> Though his face be better than any man's, yet his leg excels all
> men's, and for a hand and a foot and a body, though they be not
> to be talked on, yet they are past compare. [II.v.40–43]

After offering her own gratuitous praise of Romeo's body, the Nurse
then accuses Juliet of being lustful.

The Nurse's feelings in the matter are directly conveyed toward the
end of the scene, when she says to Juliet,

> I am the drudge, and toil in your delight,
> But you shall bear the burden soon at night.
>
> [II.v.76–77]

Her phrase "bear the burden" quibbles on the two meanings "do the
work" and "bear the weight of your lover." It is clear that this is the
work the Nurse herself would like to do instead of being the lovers'
messenger, about which she complains interminably.

The Nurse's tormenting of Juliet in this scene introduces a new aspect
of their relationship. Earlier, we saw the fondness of the older woman
for the child she had nursed. As Juliet comes of age, however, the Nurse
responds differently to her. She is a woman keenly aware of the vulnerability of the body to time. She has hardly appeared onstage, in her first
scene, before she mentions the fact that she has only four teeth left. She
is a lusty, bawdy woman—but one whose "dancing days," in Capulet's
phrase, are now gone. Like him, she feels acutely her aging, and like
him, too, she feels specifically the loss of sexual opportunity. In the
previous scene, seeking out Romeo among his friends, she was the butt
of the young men's lewd humor, trying to maintain her fancied dignity
even while Mercutio and Benvolio made fun of her. The Nurse could
recall warmly the stumbling and the first words of the toddler, but now,
as Juliet becomes an adolescent and is about to enter a sexual relationship—indeed, the news of when and where is precisely what the Nurse
withholds—the older woman becomes irritable, even cruel, toward the
younger. One of the malevolent forces in the environment surrounding
Romeo and Juliet is the envy of the old for the young—the envy of the
parental generation for the youth, vigor, and sexuality of adolescence.

Even Friar Lawrence, in his mild way, alludes with comic effect to
the sexuality of the young couple and his own status as an outsider. Like
the Nurse, he becomes a parent surrogate: they are the two adults to
whom the adolescents turn when their love for one another estranges

them from their actual parents. Arriving for the marriage ceremony, Juliet greets Friar Lawrence with a kiss. He responds that "Romeo shall thank thee, daughter, for us both," meaning that Romeo will return her kiss on his behalf. When Romeo obliges, Juliet, with a characteristic twinkle in her eye, decides that he has exceeded his assignment and included a kiss from himself, and that she must therefore restore the balance by giving him one back. Friar Lawrence realizes that he had better get on quickly with the marriage ceremony.

Juliet's playful eagerness here recalls the scene of their meeting, when the touch of their hands, and their first kiss, and then their second, were indeed, in Romeo's words, "trespass sweetly urg'd" by her. The candor and the frank welcoming of sexuality hinted at in these exchanges find their fullest expression, however, in Juliet's superb epithalamium. In this soliloquy, she anticipates her wedding night with such sensuous explicitness that Dr. Bowdler had to expurgate it heavily in order to render the play suitable for a family audience. Juliet's references to "stainless maidenhood," to "love-performing night," to "amorous rites," leave no doubt about the sexual content of her anticipation. The invocation of night is sanctioned by epithalamium tradition,[7] but Juliet's speech has an urgency and intensity which are without precedent:

> Gallop apace, you fiery-footed steeds,
> Towards Phoebus' lodging. Such a waggoner
> As Phaeton would whip you to the west
> And bring in cloudy night immediately.
> Spread thy close curtain, love-performing night,
> That runaway's eyes may wink, and Romeo
> Leap to these arms untalk'd-of and unseen.
> Lovers can see to do their amorous rites
> By their own beauties; or, if love be blind,
> It best agrees with night. Come, civil night,
> Thou sober-suited matron, all in black,
> And learn me how to lose a winning match
> Play'd for a pair of stainless maidenhoods.
> Hood my unmann'd blood, bating in my cheeks,
> With thy black mantle, till strange love grow bold,
> Think true love acted simple modesty.

7. See McGown's (1976) discussion of this tradition.

> Come night, come Romeo, come thou day in night,
> For thou wilt lie upon the wings of night
> Whiter than new snow upon a raven's back.
> Come gentle night, come loving black-brow'd night,
> Give me my Romeo; and when I shall die
> Take him and cut him out in little stars,
> And he will make the face of heaven so fine
> That all the world will be in love with night,
> And pay no worship to the garish sun.
>
> [III.ii.1–25]

Juliet's speech is charged with imperatives, repeated with increasing urgency: "Gallop apace . . . spread thy close curtain . . . come, civil night . . . come night, come Romeo, come thou day in night . . . come gentle night, come loving black-brow'd night." The terms Juliet uses to invoke night are themselves concretely evocative of sexual excitement. "Spread thy close curtain, love-performing night": other verbs could have supplied the one syllable required by the meter, but, for example, "low'r thy close curtain" would miss the sexual charge. Juliet's language in this soliloquy is dense with sexual overtone:

> Hood my unmann'd blood, bating in my cheeks,
> With thy black mantle, till strange love grow bold,
> Think true love acted simple modesty.

Unmann'd has two meanings. The first is that Juliet is as yet without a husband. The second, more technical meaning resonates with the first. The terms are borrowed from falconry: an untrained (unmanned) hawk would flutter its wings (bate) when taken out of doors unless a hood were drawn over its head. The image evokes at once Juliet's sexual inexperience and her sexual eagerness: in its technical meaning as well as its sound, blood bating in her cheeks is blood beating in her cheeks, a manifestation of the excitement that agitates, too, the rhythm of her language: "Come night, come Romeo, come thou day in night. . . ." Juliet urges night to come so that her shyness may dissipate and her unfamiliarity with love may be replaced by boldness—the boldness not of experience but of innocence, when "true love acted" is "simple modesty."

Juliet's invocation of Phaeton, in urging night to come, establishes a grim undercurrent that is at odds with what she means to say. This story foreshadows her own. The youthful Phaeton, like Romeo and Juliet, defied parental advice and insisted on a headstrong course; like theirs, it ended in disaster.[8]

Even in her sexual eagerness, Juliet reminds us of how young she is by comparing her own impatience to that of a little girl:

> So tedious is this day
> As is the night before some festival
> To an impatient child that hath new robes
> And may not wear them.
>
> [III.ii.28–31]

8. There are other allusions to Ovid's tale. Verbal similarities indicate that Shakespeare drew on Arthur Golding's (1567) translation of the *Metamorphoses,* in which the tale appears. Phaeton, son of Clymene, a mortal woman, and the sun-god Apollo, asks to be allowed to drive his father's golden sun chariot across the sky. Apollo tries to dissuade Phaeton by describing the dangers of the course he seeks to follow and the wildness of the horses that pull the chariot. He warns his son that he is but a mortal, too young and too weak. But Phaeton, "both yong in yeares and wit," would not be dissuaded. In fact, he could not control the horses, which ran wild, burning heaven and earth, until Jove threw a thunderbolt, killing the youth. Then,

> Wyth ruthfull cheere and heavie heart his father gave great mone
> And would not shew himself abrode, but mournd at hom alone.
> And if it be to be believed, as bruited is by fame
> A day did passe without the Sunne.
>
> [*Metamorphoses,* trans. Golding, lines 416–19]

Similarly, in the final scene of *Romeo and Juliet,* the Prince begins the concluding sestet,

> A glooming peace this morning with it brings:
> The sun for sorrow will not show his head.

Ironically, the wish that Juliet expresses after her wedding night to stop the coming of dawn has been fulfilled.

The story of the son seeking prerogatives that rightfully belong only to his far more powerful father—prerogatives that have to do, moreover, with controlling forces of a wild and animal nature—is one with obvious oedipal resonances. It is a cautionary tale, and expresses one of the themes I have been discussing in relation to *Romeo and Juliet*—the resistance of the parental generation to the ascendance to full power and sexuality of the next generation.

It is of interest that the father in Ovid's tale, like the adults in the play, urges his son to follow the middle course. Apollo cautions Phaeton not to drive across all five zones of the earth, but rather to stay in the center three. He warns him against going too high or too low (if too high he will burn the stars, if too low he will burn the earth), neither too far to the right nor too far to the left. Like Friar Lawrence, cautioning Romeo and Juliet to "love moderately," Apollo advises his son, "most safetie is the meane." The youthful Phaeton could no more accept this parental advice than could Romeo and Juliet.

At this point her Nurse enters. Again she has crucial information, and again she makes Juliet wait for it. Earlier, Juliet had been exasperated but polite. Now she explodes,

> What devil art thou that dost torment me thus?
> This torture should be roar'd in dismal hell.

[III.ii.43–44]

The Nurse had entered wringing her hands and wailing:

> Ah weraday, he's dead, he's dead, he's dead!
> We are undone, lady, we are undone.
> Alack the day, he's gone, he's kill'd, he's dead.

[III.ii.37–39]

Juliet understands her to be speaking of Romeo and the Nurse allows her to go on believing this, until, in her own good time, she lets fall Tybalt's name. Juliet then begins to piece together what has actually happened: Romeo has killed her cousin Tybalt and has been banished as a result.

The killing of Tybalt is the turning point of the play. It forces Juliet to choose, now definitively, between her new love and her parents. For Romeo, too, a choice is forced. Returning from their secret wedding ceremony, he is accosted by Tybalt, who attempts to provoke him verbally. Romeo, happily in love, alludes to his new kinship with Tybalt and resists the provocation, but Mercutio takes up Tybalt's challenge. A fight ensues which Romeo tries to stop, and his friend is wounded under his arm. It is only after Mercutio dies that Romeo, enraged, kills Tybalt.[9]

When Juliet learns that her husband has slain her cousin, her initial response is one of allegiance to her family. The very language she turns against Romeo, however, echoes his own, in her use, for the first time, of paradox and oxymoron:

---

9. This is another significant change introduced by Shakespeare: in Brooke's poem, Romeo kills Tybalt in self-defense. Indeed, the character of Mercutio is largely Shakespeare's invention, developed from a single reference in his source to "one cald Mercutio. / A courtier that eche where was highly had in pryce, / For hee was coorteous of his speche, and pleasant of devise" (lines 254–56). For Romeo to kill Tybalt not in self-defense, but out of loyalty to his witty, high-spirited, altogether beguiling friend, is one of Shakespeare's many innovations which deepen our sympathy with the young lovers.

Beautiful tyrant, fiend angelical,
Dove-feather'd raven, wolvish-ravening lamb!
Despised substance of divinest show!
Just opposite to what thou justly seem'st!
A damned saint, an honourable villain!

[III.ii.75–79]

The internal contradiction of these phrases mirrors that of her feelings.
But when the Nurse joins her, saying, "Shame come to Romeo," Juliet
suddenly reverses herself and springs to his defense:

Blister'd be thy tongue
For such a wish. He was not born to shame.
Upon his brow shame is asham'd to sit,
For 'tis a throne where honour may be crown'd
Sole monarch of the universal earth.
O, what a beast was I to chide at him.

[III.ii.90–95]

It is the Nurse's attack on Romeo that crystallizes Juliet's defense of
him, replacing ambivalence with conviction. As I observed in an altogether different context, in discussing Anne Frank, it is characteristic of
adolescents to try to resolve an internal conflict by externalizing it,
turning an inner struggle into one between the adolescent and a parental
figure. Now, when the Nurse chides her, "Will you speak well of him
that kill'd your cousin?" Juliet replies, "Shall I speak ill of him that is
my husband?" Juliet counterposes the conflicting loyalties directly, stating
that Romeo's banishment is harder for her to bear than the deaths of
both parents. At this point, momentarily, she has an impulse to turn
back to them ("Where is my father and my mother, Nurse?") before she
commits herself, irrevocably, to Romeo.

When next we see Romeo and Juliet, it is the dawn after their wedding
night. Juliet speaks first. She who had been so impatient for time to pass
when she was waiting for the Nurse to bring word from Romeo, imploring day to end and her wedding night to come, now tries to stop
the passage of time. Juliet, who had been the more realistic and down-
to-earth, now tries to persuade herself and Romeo that the bird they
hear is a nightingale and not a lark, that the light breaking in the east
is not the dawn. Her denial is phrased in the kind of extravagant flight
that had earlier marked Romeo's speech:

> Yond light is not daylight, I know it, I.
> It is some meteor that the sun exhales
> To be to thee this night a torchbearer
> And light thee on thy way to Mantua.
> Therefore stay yet: thou need'st not to be gone.
>
> [III.v.12–16]

But when Romeo begins to join her in wishful fantasy, she once more becomes realistic, and acknowledges that

> It is the lark that sings so out of tune,
> Straining harsh discord and unpleasing sharps.
>
> [III.v.27–28]

As it has been in each of their meetings, their colloquy is interrupted by the Nurse. This time she is coming to warn Juliet that her mother is on her way to her chamber. Romeo leaves, to his banishment in Mantua, and her mother enters. She has come to deliver Capulet's "decree" that Juliet is to be married three days hence to Paris.

For Capulet to issue such a decree—the word is his—represents a sudden and puzzling change. In an earlier scene, he had acknowledged his reluctance to lose his only remaining child to marriage but had resolved, in the end, to respect her own wishes:

> But woo her, gentle Paris, get her heart,
> My will to her consent is but a part,
> And she agreed, within her scope of choice
> Lies my consent and fair according voice.
>
> [I.ii.16–19]

Now he reverses himself. He himself comments on the "haste" of his action, and we are offered no convincing explanation for it. It is not that he is responding to pressure from Paris. The two men have been conversing about the death of Tybalt and the fact that, therefore, there has been no opportunity for Paris to press his suit. The hour is late and Paris has already taken his leave when Capulet suddenly calls him back:

> Sir Paris, I will make a desperate tender
> Of my child's love. I think she will be rul'd
> In all respects by me; nay, more, I doubt it not.
>
> [III.iv.12–14]

The explanation offered by Lady Capulet—that he is setting the wedding date three days hence in order to end Juliet's mourning for Tybalt—makes little sense. We come closer to an understanding, I believe, if we consider the change in Capulet to be one of the ways in which the events of the play mirror the inner experience of adolescence. The parents are often seen to be arbitrary, capricious, and controlling in order to ease and justify the necessary but difficult process of separation. Juliet has taken a momentous step in secretly marrying Romeo, the enemy of her family, and in having consummated their marriage. She casts her lot with her new husband rather than with her family when the choice is forced by the death of Tybalt. Now, her father behaves as if he knows what she has done. He changes in ways commensurate with the change in Juliet.

We have a measure of the estrangement between Juliet and her parents in the scene between Juliet and Lady Capulet. Their colloquy, especially juxtaposed to Juliet's parting from Romeo, is stiff and formal. The language they use is artificial, with wordplay and repetition directing attention to words themselves rather than expressing feeling. Assuming that Juliet is weeping over Tybalt's death, her mother advises her to "have done" and indicates that there are correct limits within which grief should be contained. Evidently those who "love moderately" must grieve moderately as well.

> *Lady Cap.* Evermore weeping for your cousin's death?
>   What, wilt thou wash him from his grave with tears?
>   And if thou couldst, thou couldst not make him live.
>   Therefore have done: some grief shows much of love,
>   But much of grief shows still some want of wit.
> *Juliet.* Yet let me weep for such a feeling loss.
> *Lady Cap.* So shall you feel the loss but not the friend
>   Which you weep for.
> *Juliet.*   Feeling so the loss,
>   I cannot choose but ever weep the friend.
>
> [III.v.69–77]

Similarly, when her father chides her for mourning excessively he begins, "In one little body / Thou counterfeits a bark, a sea, a wind," and then goes on, point by point, to explain the simile. The self-consciousness of their language in these exchanges is an index of the emotional estrangement between Juliet and her parents.

This estrangement is most directly represented in Juliet's conversation with her mother. Juliet seems to say one thing, but privately means another. When Lady Capulet speaks of "that villain Romeo," Juliet replies,

> O, how my heart abhors
> To hear him nam'd, and cannot come to him
> To wreak the love I bore my cousin
> Upon his body that hath slaughter'd him.
>
> [III.v.99–102]

The layers of deception and equivocation are multiple. She says to her mother that she abhors to hear Romeo named, and then adds, for herself, that she abhors to hear him named and be unable to come to him. Her statement again becomes a lie when she adds that she would come to him to avenge her cousin's death. But there is still another, private meaning in her reference to the love that she would wreak upon Romeo's body. Juliet pretends to converse with her mother, but her statements are equivocations and asides whose true meaning is hidden.

When her mother announces to Juliet her father's plan that she is to marry Paris three days hence, Juliet refuses, then continues her equivocation:

> I pray you tell my lord and father, madam,
> I will not marry yet. And when I do, I swear
> It shall be Romeo, whom you know I hate,
> Rather than Paris.
>
> [III.v.120–23]

At this point Capulet enters and asks his wife whether she has "deliver'd to her our decree." She replies, "Ay sir, but she will none," and he echoes incredulously, "How? Will she none?" It seems long ago that Juliet asked of her mother, "Madam, what is your will?"

Now, Juliet asserts her own will, although she tries to maintain a conciliatory tone with her father. This seems only to inflame him. His wife tries to intervene, but Capulet continues his attack on his daughter:

> Hang thee young baggage, disobedient wretch!
> I tell thee what—get thee to church a Thursday
> Or never after look me in the face.
> Speak not, reply not, do not answer me.
> My fingers itch. Wife, we scarce thought us blest

That God had lent us but this only child;
But now I see this one is one too much,
And that we have a curse in having her.

[III.v.160–67]

The Nurse, too, tries to intercede, but his anger is uncontrollable. He threatens to throw Juliet out of his house and let her die if she will not submit to his will.

Graze where you will, you shall not house with me.
Look to't, think on't, I do not use to jest.
Thursday is near. Lay hand on heart. Advise.
And you be mine I'll give you to my friend;
And you be not, hang! Beg! Starve! Die in the streets!
For by my soul I'll ne'er acknowledge thee,
Nor what is mine shall never do thee good.
Trust to't, bethink you. I'll not be forsworn.

[III.v.188–95]

Lady Capulet withdraws from the struggle, and Juliet turns to the Nurse, "Comfort me, counsel me." The Nurse, however, quickly assesses where expedience lies and reverses herself. She advises:

Then, since the case so stands as now it doth,
I think it best you married with the County.
O, he's a lovely gentleman.
Romeo's a dishclout to him. An eagle, madam,
Hath not so green, so quick, so fair an eye
As Paris hath. Beshrew my very heart,
I think you are happy in this second match,
For it excels your first;

[III.v.216–23]

With this, Juliet's estrangement from the Nurse becomes complete. She says with quiet irony, "Well, thou has comforted me marvellous much," and proceeds to lie to her. Only after she has dismissed her does Juliet speak freely, now calling the Nurse an "ancient damnation": "Thou and my bosom henceforth shall be twain." Thus we see, one by one, the separation of Juliet from each of her parental figures until, at the end, Friar Lawrence flees and she is left, in the tomb, entirely alone.

Capulet's fury against Juliet, which prompts his wife and even his servant to challenge him, has mounted finally to unbridled rage. "And you be mine," he thunders, "I'll give you to my friend." The issue is whether Juliet is indeed "his" and therefore to be given to his friend. Were Juliet to accept the man designated by her father, marriage would not be a separation from him but an exertion of his will and an extension of their bond. For her refusal to accept these terms, he threatens her finally with death.

The rage of Capulet against his beloved daughter commands our attention and points to a significant theme. In this play about adolescence, the most passionate relations, besides that of Romeo and Juliet, are the feelings of a parent for the child of the opposite sex. It is out of the struggle against these ties that the love of Romeo and Juliet develops. Lady Montague plays a minor role, but what is suggested of her feeling for Romeo mirrors that which is more fully presented in the relation of Capulet to Juliet. In Lady Montague's only appearance onstage, at the beginning of the play, she barely allows Benvolio to finish his account of the street fight that has just taken place before asking: "O where is Romeo, saw you him today? / Right glad I am he was not at this fray" (I.i.114–15). Lady Montague does not appear again, but we hear of her at the play's end: her husband reports that she has died of grief on learning that her son has been banished.[10]

Capulet's special tenderness for his daughter is also immediately apparent in the scene in which he is introduced. He responds to Paris's suit by emphasizing Juliet's youthfulness and inexperience of life, and indicates his reluctance that she marry just yet. At first he speaks only of Juliet herself—she is still just a child, too young to marry. But in the next lines there is a shift. Now the father alludes to his own need for his daughter.

> Earth hath swallowed all my hopes but she;
> She is the hopeful lady of my earth.

It has already been emphasized that Capulet is an old man; now we learn that Juliet is his only surviving child. The brief but powerful allusion to the deaths of his other children suggests the importance this daughter must have for her father. The repetition of the word *hope*—indeed, the very use of the word *hope* as a synonym for *children*—sharpens the

10. Similarly, in *Othello* Desdemona's father, Brabantio, dies of grief over the marriage of his daughter.

poignancy of his statement. These few lines establish the father's tenderness and protectiveness toward his daughter—and also his reluctance to let go his only remaining "hope." This reluctance turns to furious determination when his heretofore obedient daughter will no longer submit to his will. He would rather she die than choose her own husband—and in so choosing, separate from him.

Juliet, estranged now from the parental figures to whom, at the outset, she had been the docile and submissive daughter, turns in desperation to another parent surrogate, Friar Lawrence. At his cell, she meets Paris—it is their only encounter in the play—and engages with him in a dialogue of stiff formality. Once Paris has gone, the spontaneity of her speech returns as she beseeches the Friar in urgent monosyllables,

> O shut the door, and when thou hast done so,
> Come weep with me, past hope, past cure, past help!
>
> [IV.i.44–45]

Friar Lawrence sets forth the plan of the sleeping potion that will mimic death: once Juliet is lain in her family tomb, Romeo, who will have been notified of the plan by messenger, will take her from there to Mantua and thus circumvent plans for the wedding to Paris.

Juliet returns now to her family, pretending a childlike obedience. She claims to have repented "the sin of disobedient opposition" to her father and begs his forgiveness, concluding, "Henceforth I am ever rul'd by you." Her father is taken in and delighted by this pretense. He says to his daughter, kneeling down before him, "This is well. Stand up. / This is as't should be." He is in an ebullient mood: rejuvenated by his daughter's apparent submission, he plans to stay up all night making preparations for the wedding. He ends the scene by reiterating his satisfaction in the return to an earlier state:

> My heart is wondrous light
> Since this same wayward girl is so reclaim'd.
>
> [IV.ii.46–47]

Juliet's duplicity in relation to her father is followed by a similar duplicity toward her mother and her Nurse as she dismisses them from her chamber on the eve of what they believe to be her wedding to Paris.

Alone now, and contemplating drinking the potion, Juliet becomes frightened. She has a momentary impulse to turn back once more to her parental figures ("I'll call them back again to comfort me"). She begins, in fact, to call the Nurse before reminding herself, "My dismal scene I needs must act alone." So disillusioned is she with adults at this point, that one of her fears before drinking the potion is that perhaps it is truly poison, and that the Friar wants her dead in order to protect himself from dishonour at having married her and Romeo. It is only the fact that "he hath still been tried a holy man" that allows her to dismiss this thought.

Then, in a moving soliloquy, she conjures up the terrors of awakening alone in the Capulet tomb:

> How if, when I am laid into the tomb,
> I wake before the time that Romeo
> Come to redeem me? There's a fearful point!
> Shall I not then be stifled in the vault,
> To whose foul mouth no healthsome air breathes in,
> And there die strangled ere my Romeo comes?
> Or, if I live, is it not very like,
> The horrible conceit of death and night
> Together with the terror of the place,
> As in a vault, an ancient receptacle
> Where for this many hundred years the bones
> Of all my buried ancestors are pack'd,
> Where bloody Tybalt yet but green in earth
> Lies festering in his shroud; where, as they say,
> At some hours in the night spirits resort—
> Alack, alack! Is it not like that I
> So early waking, what with loathsome smells,
> And shrieks like mandrakes torn out of the earth,
> That living mortals, hearing them, run mad—
> O, if I wake, shall I not be distraught,
> Environed with all these hideous fears,
> And madly play with my forefathers' joints,
> And pluck the mangled Tybalt from his shroud,
> And, in this rage, with some great kinsman's bone
> As with a club dash out my desperate brains?
>
> [IV.iii.30–54]

The question she begins in line 36 ("is it not very like . . .") is broken off and begun again in line 45 ("Is it not like that I . . ."). The sentence is not completed until line 54, sustained over nearly twenty lines as a profusion of macabre, terrifying images press themselves upon her imagination. So vividly does she evoke the ghastly sights, the sounds, the loathsome smells of the tomb that in her frenzy she begins to see the ghost of Tybalt before her. In the final line her desperation bursts through metric constraints as in spite of all she has imagined she drinks the contents of the vial:

> Stay, Tybalt, stay!
> Romeo, Romeo, Romeo, here's drink! I drink to thee!
> [IV.iii.57–58]

The solitary courage of Juliet's act is emphasized by its juxtaposition with the next scene, in which her mother, father, and Nurse are bustling about, getting dates and quinces for the pastry, preparing for the wedding feast. With his daughter seemingly obedient to his will, Capulet continues to be in an expansive mood, affectionately urging the Nurse—now "good Angelica"—to spare no cost. Again he makes reference to the prowess of his youth, but this time without the mournful tone that had earlier accompanied such thoughts. It is three o'clock in the morning, but Capulet feels he can stay up all night; after all, he did so many times in the past and never fell sick then—what is to stop him now?

The Nurse is sent to waken Juliet in a scene with ironic parallels to the earlier scene when she had been sent to fetch the girl; she calls to Juliet using the same terms of endearment. This time, however, she finds her seemingly dead. Mother, father, and Paris join the Nurse in a formal chorus of mourning before Juliet is carried off to the Capulet tomb.

The messenger who had been sent to Mantua by Friar Lawrence to inform Romeo of the plan is detained because of a quarantine, and instead Romeo is told by his servant that Juliet is dead. He rushes to the Capulet tomb, where, with words that echo Juliet's own, Romeo drinks the poison he had obtained. Friar Lawrence, learning of the misfiring of his plan, hurries to the tomb and enters it just as Juliet begins to waken. They hear sounds that indicate the approach of the Watch. Frightened, Friar Lawrence urges Juliet to flee with him, but she refuses.

Thus having dismissed the last of her parental figures, Juliet is, at the end, entirely alone. She kisses Romeo's lips, which are still warm, hoping that some drop of poison still remains "to help her after." Again there are sounds of the Watch and, seizing Romeo's dagger, Juliet stabs herself and dies. At the end, as at the beginning, the two families enter, followed by the Prince, and we return from the private world of the young lovers to the world of their parents against which their love developed.

CHAPTER SIX

Late Adolescence:
Persuasion

Virginia Woolf observed of Jane Austen that of all great writers she is the most difficult to catch in the act of greatness. Of the hilarious burlesque "Love and Freindship," which Jane Austen wrote when she was only fourteen,[1] Woolf wrote,

Undoubtedly, the story must have roused the schoolroom to uproarious laughter. And yet, nothing is more obvious than that this girl ... sitting in her private corner of the common parlour, was writing not to draw a laugh from brother and sisters, and not for home consumption. She was writing for everybody, for nobody, for our age, for her own; in other words, even at that early age Jane Austen was writing [1925, p. 139].

It was not only her astonishingly accomplished juvenilia that she wrote amid the conviviality of the common parlor. Jane Austen's nephew, in his memoir,[2] described his aunt writing the novels of her maturity in the family sitting room, where she was subject to all kinds of casual interruption, taking care that her occupation should not be suspected by servants or visitors, or anyone beyond her own family. She wrote on small sheets of paper that could easily be put away or covered, and requested that a creaky door not be fixed so that she might have warning should anyone approach. In *A Room of One's Own*, Woolf remarks on the furtiveness of this enterprise; she takes the scene described by the nephew and makes it a metaphor for the situation of the woman writer through history, lacking a room of her own in which to seek refuge from the claims of daily life, and where the privacy of the imagination may find expression.

---

1. The title retains her fourteen-year-old spelling.
2. James Austen-Leigh, *A Memoir of Jane Austen,* 1870.

The picture of Jane Austen writing epitomizes the intrinsic conflict between the demands of creative work and those of familial responsibility, between solitude and engagement. It is not a uniquely feminine predicament, but the conflict is heightened for a woman, whose "place" traditionally has been defined precisely by her availability and responsiveness to others. Austen's subject matter, too, is deeply rooted in the situation of women in her time, and similarly reaches beyond these particulars. She wrote novels about courtship, which end in marriage. The novels are entertaining, but the seriousness of her subject cannot be too greatly stressed: Jane Austen was writing about the only decision a female could make. Marriage is the traditional ending of comedy, but marriage in the life of a woman was a serious matter, an economic necessity: there was little else a middle- or upper-class woman could do to support herself, and she could not inherit property.[3] In this economic context, as Cooley (1981) points out, her heroines live in a world in which "their only real chance to determine their own fate is to say yes or no wisely to a proposal of marriage."

Jane Austen wrote about young women taking their place in the social order in the only way that was then open to them: her subject was the transition to adulthood. The array of alternatives open to women has of course vastly widened between her time and our own, and the decisions that must be made toward the close of adolescence are correspondingly more numerous and complex. A choice of lifework, whether to marry or not, whether to have children or not (if so, how many, and when), an explicit sexuality—this richness of possibilities was not a dilemma facing Jane Austen, nor her heroines. In the final chapter on the resolution of adolescence I nonetheless turn to a novel by Jane Austen because this work so masterfully renders internal processes of development that remain constant in spite of profound historical and cultural change.

Persuasion, Jane Austen's last completed novel, is an exception to most generalizations about her work. "Always a lady," wrote a scholar who was influential in the rise of her critical fortunes.[4] It is a point on which her nineteenth-century admirers and critics agreed. Here, for example, is Charlotte Brontë's affronted reaction to *Emma*:

---

3. In two of Austen's six novels, an estate is entailed on a distant male relative in the absence of a son; in a third, an inheritance is bequeathed to a son at the expense of two daughters and their mother.

4. This was the Shakespeare scholar, Richard Simpson, who, writing in 1870, was among the first to recognize Austen's ironic relation to her subject matter.

the Passions are perfectly unknown to her; she rejects even a speaking acquaintance with that stormy Sisterhood; even to the Feelings she vouchsafes no more than an occasional graceful but distant recognition . . . Jane Austen was a complete and most sensible lady, but a very incomplete, and rather insensible (not senseless) woman [In Southam (1968), p. 128].

This view of Jane Austen will not be supported by *Persuasion*.

The "light, and bright, and sparkling"[5] quality at the surface of the other novels is all but absent here. Rather, the tone is mournful, elegiac—and its mournfulness is not fully dissipated by the happy ending that convention requires. It is the story of a young woman of twenty-seven who is to a large degree absorbed in looking back to a decision she made when she was nineteen. Then, she had yielded to persuasion and rejected the man she loved. Anne Elliot has changed in the intervening years, and she is given the opportunity of making the choice a second time. This time she chooses differently.

My interest is in the changes within Anne that make it possible, now, for her to choose differently. The narrative technique of *Persuasion* makes it well suited to this inquiry. Unlike the novels which depend more upon satire for their pleasure, and which set the characters off at a distance for our amusement, *Persuasion* draws us into the inner world of its heroine. The novel takes its grave and tender tone from her mood; the events of the novel, and the characters around her, are presented to us largely from her point of view. Through her eyes we see Frederick Wentworth when chance returns him to her small world after an absence of more than seven years. The reader is given no privileged access to knowledge of his feelings but must make inferences, as Anne does, from his behavior—from the series of actions that suggest, by increasing degrees, the return of his regard and finally of his love for her. Much of the change within Anne has taken place before the novel opens, but in her melancholy state the past is so much present that we are told a good deal, and can infer more, about the younger Anne. Between the ages of nineteen and twenty-seven, Anne has become able to move away from the family of her childhood, both literally and figuratively, toward the commitments of her adulthood. Her growth, and the choices presented to her, exemplify central issues in late adolescent development: the dif-

5. The words are her own, describing *Pride and Prejudice* in a letter to her sister Cassandra.

ference between Anne at twenty-seven and Anne at nineteen is that she has relinquished, finally, her submissive relation to the authority of a parental figure and has come into possession of her own authority.

Her maturation requires that she leave the narrow world of her family to find her place in a broader social world. Jane Austen has been variously praised, criticized, and patronized for the narrowness of her social purview,[6] but again, this novel is an exception. Over its course she offers her heroine a widening social world within which she finds alternative ways of living to that of her family. In this wider world, Anne becomes aware of other perspectives on herself than that to which she is accustomed; she discovers, too, other possibilities for what she, as a woman, may become.

Persuasion opens in Kellynch-hall, ancestral home of the Elliot family, with Sir Walter Elliot taking up the only book he ever reads, the *Baronetage*. Here he can peruse, yet again, the history of his own family, for it is at this page that the favored volume obligingly falls open. A quotation from the *Baronetage* serves to sketch the family history and to introduce the present occupants of Kellynch-hall, Sir Walter and his daughters, Elizabeth and Anne. Lady Elliot is dead, and a third daughter, Mary, has married and lives in Uppercross.

It is Anne Elliot who will be the focus of our interest. Anne, we are told, possessed "an elegance of mind and sweetness of character, which must have placed her high with any people of real understanding." Her family, however, are not such people. Her father, foolishly vain and self-absorbed, cares only for rank and fine personal appearance, "and the Sir Walter Elliot, who united these gifts, was the constant object of his warmest respect and devotion." His narcissistic delight extends so far as to include his eldest daughter, Elizabeth, "very handsome and very like himself," but Anne, the middle child, so unlike him in every way, is excluded from this charmed circle. Time, Sir Walter regrets to see, is wearing down the looks of those around him; only he and Elizabeth seem immune to its ravages.

Sir Walter's insistence on living in a style commensurate with his inflated self-importance has led him to financial embarrassment. He and Elizabeth consider ways to retrench (Anne is not consulted), but finally

6. "Three or four Families in a Country Village is the very thing to work on," she advised her young niece, beginning her own experiments in fiction.

even Sir Walter must acknowledge that simply cutting back on charity will not be a sufficient economy to meet his debts. Reluctantly, then, he consents to adopt the only course open to him: Kellynch-hall must be let.

The year is 1814. The end of the Napoleonic wars was returning naval officers to England's shores, and Sir Walter's solicitor advises him that "they will all be wanting a home." A navy man, he urges, would be an ideal tenant, and with his assistance arrangements are concluded for Kellynch-hall to be rented to an Admiral and Mrs. Croft. It is thus that Anne comes to meet again, at twenty-seven, the man she had earlier rejected, for Frederick Wentworth, the man with whom she had fallen in love at nineteen, is the brother of Mrs. Croft.

At the beginning of the novel, then, Anne is thrust from her parental home: over its course, she grows away from the rootedness in the past that is symbolized by Kellynch-hall toward a more uncertain but more liberating future. The renting of the ancestral home to Admiral and Mrs. Croft establishes a tension in the novel between what the landed gentry represents and other possibilities represented by the navy. The opening description of Sir Walter turning to the *Baronetage* not only establishes his absurd self-absorption, but also has an undercurrent of boredom, depletion, and exhaustion. Indeed, in conversation with his solicitor he insists on understanding the word *gentleman* to mean only a man of property, a sense that was already archaic at the time the novel is set.

> Sir Walter Elliot, of Kellynch-hall, in Somersetshire, was a man who, for his own amusement, never took up any book but the Baronetage; there he found occupation for an idle hour, and con-solation in a distressed one; there his faculties were roused into admiration and respect, by contemplating the limited remnant of the earliest patents; there any unwelcome sensations, arising from domestic affairs, changed naturally into pity and contempt, as he turned over the almost endless creations of the last century—and there, if every other leaf were powerless, he could read his own history with an interest which never failed. . . . [p. 35]

Sir Walter's faculties, apparently, require some rousing. The naval officers, in contrast, are full of energy and vitality, their lives dense with event. Sir Walter's absorbed contemplation of the history of his forefathers underlines the fact that what the landed gentry possess has come to them passively, through inheritance; what the navy men possess they have acquired by their own exertions.[7]

The "heartless elegance" of the class personified by Sir Walter is counterposed, throughout, to the straightforwardness and lack of affectation of the naval officers. When Anne meets Captain and Mrs. Harville in their rented lodgings in Lyme, their hospitality strikes her as "so unlike the usual style of give-and-take invitations, and dinners of formality and display." "Only those who invite from the heart," Anne thinks, could think rooms so small capable of accommodating all of the party to whom the Harvilles warmly opened their home. Modest though it is, their cottage is filled with Captain Harville's own carvings in wood and with curiosities collected from the distant countries he had visited. Far from having belonged to the family for generations, the Harvilles' lodgings are temporary, not even their own—yet in a sense made their own by objects of personal associations gathered in their travels. These belongings suggest a wider world than that backward-looking one in which Anne has been raised, and an alternative way of living, both remote and desirable.

At sea, the ties of rank and property that bind each generation to the previous generation are broken. As Sir Walter observes with distaste, in the navy one may be shunned by someone whose father one's own father would not have spoken to. At that time the navy, as he accurately comments, was the means of bringing persons of obscure birth to distinction, "and raising men to honours which their fathers and grandfathers never dreamt of." Historical changes were taking place, and Sir Walter, as a representative of the old order, shudders to see them. The social mobility that became possible in the navy meant that each generation was not bound to repeat the life of the generation before. These historical changes, which form the background for the events of the novel, also mirror the psychological processes that concern me here—the loosening of the bonds to the previous generation that constitutes the essential developmental task of adolescence.

Anne Elliot as we first meet her, like Sir Walter reading the *Baronetage,* is tied to the past. What she sees, looking back, is loss. The present time of the novel is the summer of 1814, but Anne is riveted on the

---

7. As background to the novel, it is important to know that a man could make his fortune in the navy: prize money was given for the capture of enemy vessels during wartime, offering rich rewards for officers.

summer of 1806 and the events that were to follow some months later. It was then that Frederick Wentworth had come into the country, having just been made a commander in consequence of the action off St. Domingo. Young, vigorous, charming, he was brimming with confidence in his own abilities and in Providence. The two had met and fallen in love, and there followed "a short period of exquisite felicity." But as Captain Wentworth then had no fortune and no certainty of obtaining one—in fact had "nothing but himself to recommend him"—Anne was persuaded to break off the engagement. Frederick Wentworth left the country and returned to the seas, angry and disappointed.

At nineteen, Anne had been "an extremely pretty girl, with gentleness, modesty, taste and feeling." Now, her bloom is gone. Indeed, when Captain Wentworth returns to the country seven years later and they meet again, he declares—not within Anne's hearing, but the remark is kindly repeated to her by her sister Mary—that he would not have recognized her, so altered is she. His word is taken up and repeated, echoing within Anne:

> "Altered beyond his knowledge!" Anne fully submitted, in silent, deep mortification. Doubtless it was so; and she could take no revenge, for he was not altered, or not for the worse. She had already acknowledged it to herself, and she could not think differently, let him think of her as he would. No; the years which had destroyed her youth and bloom had only given him a more glowing, manly, open look, in no respect lessening his personal advantages. She had seen the same Frederick Wentworth.
>
> "So altered that he should not have known her again!" These were words which could not but dwell with her. . . . He had thought her wretchedly altered. . . . [pp. 85–86]

Anne has become an onlooker at life, no longer a participant. It is she who sits at the piano, playing while the others dance. When the question is asked whether she herself does not dance, the answer given is: "Oh! no, never; she has quite given up dancing. She had rather play." The pleasures of life are muted for Anne; as summer fades, it is in the autumn landscape that she finds something like satisfaction, seeing there a reflection of her own melancholy state.

What Jane Austen has given us is a young woman who has remained in mourning. The passing of years has not diminished her suffering, nor its effects, visible in "the ruins of her face." Faded and thin, saying little and little noticed, Anne moves through hours and days in her familial home that have little to vary their sameness. With "every enjoyment of youth clouded," Anne's bloom has been destroyed. The metaphor is reiterated in the text and in the setting of the novel: its landscape of "tawny leaves and withered hedges" is that of Anne's inner world. Her mood colors the narrative and gives it its elegiac tone. Even an excursion to the lively seaside resort of Lyme is set in November, and finds the streets empty, the hotels abandoned, "scarcely any family but of the residents left." The pleasant little bay, which in season is animated with bathing machines and people, now is deserted. The description of the surrounding countryside continues on the same mournful note: "above all, Pinny, with its green chasms between romantic rocks, where the scattered forest trees and orchards of luxuriant growth declare that many a generation must have passed away since the first partial falling of the cliff prepared the ground for such a state . . ." (p. 117). We see the scene as Anne sees it: the sight of luxuriant orchards evokes thoughts of earlier generations that have died.

Indeed, the sheer density of mourners who people this work must make clear that mourning is one of its principal subjects. To begin, the brief history of the Elliot family, presented in the opening paragraph of the novel as a quotation from the *Baronetage,* makes reference to two deaths, that of Lady Elliot and of a stillborn son. Sir Walter, then, is a widower, as is Mr. William Walter Elliot, the cousin on whom his estate is entailed in the absence of a surviving son. Mr. Elliot, who has been estranged from the rest of the family for some years, reappears first as a mysterious stranger in Lyme, when he and his servant are identified six times in the space of two pages by the fact that they are in mourning. The family's close friend, Lady Russell, is a widow, and so is Mrs. Smith, Anne's school chum, whom she discovers in Bath living in reduced circumstances since the death of her husband. We witness directly the grieving of Mrs. Musgrove, mother-in-law of Anne's younger sister Mary, for her son who died at sea.

There is another mourner who figures prominently in the novel. This is Captain Benwick, whose fiancée Fanny has died. From the first, Anne sees his situation as parallel to her own, but she intuits, correctly, that his mourning will follow a very different course. We know precisely when Fanny died, to the month; indeed, we are in many cases told exactly how much time has passed since a loss occurred. It is thirteen years since the death of Lady Elliot, less than a year that Mr. Elliot is a widower, two years since the death of Mrs. Smith's husband, two years since Dick Musgrove died—and over seven years since Anne lost Captain Wentworth. It is of crucial importance that these times be fixed, because a central issue in this work is how long mourning does—and should—last.

When we first meet Captain Benwick, during the excursion to Lyme, it is November. His fiancée had died the previous June, but as he was away at sea, the news of her death did not reach him until August. Only three months have passed since he learned of Fanny's death, but the mourning of Captain Benwick is presented from the first with more than a touch of irony. The history of his private life, we are told, "rendered him perfectly interesting in the eyes of all the ladies"—as though he were a circulating library novel. "He had a pleasing face and a melancholy air, just as he ought to have." The insistence on the social response to Captain Benwick—whether the ladies found him interesting, what sort of an air he ought to have—sets him at a distance, unlike Anne, whose grief we are made to feel. The melancholy of Captain Benwick has an edge of self-conscious savoring, as he cites Byron and Scott for images of undying love. He brings to mind the early Romeo, in love as much with love's literary tradition as with Rosaline. The poems that Captain Benwick speaks of earnestly to Anne—"Giaour" and "The Bride of Abydos," "Marmion" and "The Lady of the Lake"—were immense popular successes at the time. But Fanny is mourned, too, by her brother, Captain Harville: his silent grief contrasts with the poetical despondence of Captain Benwick. We are meant not to trust the strength of Benwick's attachment to the dead Fanny, and indeed it is not long before it is replaced by another.

Anne Elliot, however, has remained faithful to her lost love in the years that have passed; for her no other attachment has replaced this one. Although physically absent, Captain Wentworth has remained continuously present in her inner world. Early in the novel, before we know anything of their connection, we are present, with Anne, at a discussion between her father and his solicitor about the prospective tenants of Kellynch-hall, Admiral and Mrs. Croft. Amid the speculation about them, Anne shows herself oddly knowledgeable about a man she has never met, quietly offering in conversation that Admiral Croft is a rear admiral of the white, that he was in the Trafalgar action, and that he has been stationed in the East Indies for several years. It takes some flattery and cajoling before her father agrees to proceed with the negotiations, and at last Anne can leave the room "to seek the comfort of cool air for her flushed cheeks; and as she walked along a favourite grove, said, with a gentle sigh, 'a few months more, and *he* perhaps, may be walking here' " (p. 54). The use of the pronoun *he,* rather than a name, is surprising here—and noteworthy, because at this point the reader does not yet know who "he" is. In the privacy of solitary reflection, it is not necessary that Anne name Frederick Wentworth: there can be, it is implied, only one italicized *he*. The omission of the name suggests the intensity of Anne's ongoing preoccupation, in which conversation with others is merely an interruption.

Over the intervening years, Anne has followed from a distance the career of Frederick Wentworth, as well as that of his brother-in-law. Her detailed knowledge indicates how carefully she has studied the navy lists, learning there what ships Captain Wentworth commanded, following their victories through the Napoleonic wars, and able, from these bare facts, to make inferences about his own fortunes. He would, she supposed, be a rich man now. Only three people in her small circle were aware of their brief engagement: what she knows of her lost love can only reflect her own alertness and the intensity of her need to remain in contact with him in fantasy.

Some clinical observations about mourning are relevant here. After the death of someone beloved, there is a powerful resistance to believing fully in the finality of the loss. This is especially true at the beginning: it is only through a gradual and painful process that the irrevocable nature of the loss is ultimately accepted. In his classic essay "Mourning and Melancholia" Freud (1917) explicated this process. There is a protracted period of painful remembering; through the cumulative experience of recognizing, in piecemeal fashion, all that will never come again, the bereaved adult becomes reconciled, over time, to the fact that what has been lost will never return. In a child or young adolescent whose parent has died, however, the wishful fantasy of preserving the lost object is more intractible.[8] It is for this reason that often the familiar signs of grief are not apparent; weeping is curtailed and the child tries to act as if life were to go on as usual. Unconsciously, and often consciously as

8. There is a rich psychoanalytic literature on mourning in childhood. I refer the reader to Bowlby, 1961, 1963; Jacobson, 1965; Wolfenstein, 1966, 1969; Nagera, 1970; Furman, 1974. The literature on the death of a parent during adolescence is more limited: see Fleming, 1963; Laufer, 1966; and again, Wolfenstein, 1966.

well, the child maintains the belief that the parent is still alive—living, perhaps, in some faraway place—and harbors persistent fantasies of a future reunion. The plot of *Persuasion* is the realization of this fantasy: after Anne has lost Frederick Wentworth, seemingly forever, fate returns him to her and this time, in the end, they are united.

There is another loss, however, whose irrevocability does not yield to fantasy. This is the death of Anne's mother, which happened, it is stated, when Anne was fourteen years old. Although very little is said about Lady Elliot herself, there is repeated reference in the opening chapter to the interval since she died. "Thirteen years had passed away since Lady Elliot's death"—as if the years themselves had died. "Thirteen years had seen [Elizabeth] mistress of Kellynch-hall . . . for thirteen years she had been doing the honours. . . . Thirteen winters revolving frosts . . . and thirteen springs." The number of years is reiterated and yet, significantly, there is nevertheless an ambiguity about just when the loss occurred.

Sir Walter has made two emendations in the printed text of the *Baronetage,* by "adding after the date of Mary's birth 'married, Dec. 16, 1810' and by inserting most accurately the day of the month on which he had lost his wife." This date is withheld in the narrative—and it is the only date so withheld, amid the profusion of dates crowding the opening paragraph. All others are given precisely, dates of birth and dates of marriage, even the birthdate of the stillborn son who will never again be mentioned:

> Elliot of Kellynch-hall
> Walter Elliot, born March 1, 1760, married, July 15, 1784, Eliza-
> beth, daughter of James Stevenson, Esq. of South Park, in the county
> of Gloucester; by which lady (who died 1800) he has issue Elizabeth,
> born June 1, 1785; Anne, born August 9, 1787; a still-born son,
> Nov. 5, 1789; Mary, born Nov. 20, 1791. [p. 35]

We are given the year in which Lady Elliot died, and we are told that Anne was then fourteen—but these two facts are mutually contradictory. If Anne was born on August 9, 1787, she would have been either twelve or thirteen when her mother died, depending when in the year the death occurred, but she could not have been fourteen.

The point of this arithmetic is to suggest that it is not altogether clear *when* Anne's mourning began. The narrative explicitly connects the early fading of her bloom to the loss of Wentworth, but Anne has suffered two losses, one at nineteen and the other at some time in early adolescence. At nineteen, she had been unable to accept Frederick Wentworth, and subsequently she has been unable to relinquish him. Like a child whose parent has died, she has kept him alive in fantasy. They are separated, seemingly forever, and yet Anne has intently followed the events of his life in those faraway places where she can never join him. The loss of Wentworth was one that she precipitated herself, by sending away the man she loved; the loss of her mother she had had no choice but to endure, passively and helplessly. In her mind Anne continues, more than seven years later, to go over and over her reasons for having acted as she did; however painful these reflections, the very question of whether or not she was justified in her decision affirms her own active part in bringing about this loss—unlike the first.

Anne's mother had died when she was twelve, or thirteen, or fourteen. Again, some clinical observations are relevant: the death of a parent during this period complicates and often interferes with the thrust of adolescent development in specific ways. While the task of the adolescent is to relinquish the idealization of the parent in order to become free for other attachments, the need of the child of adolescent whose parent has died is the opposite: it is to idealize the dead. Enshrined in memory, the lost parent is preserved. Uncorrected by the experience of day-to-day reality, the image of the lost parent is enhanced by wishful fantasy and becomes, therefore, even more difficult to relinquish. There is a strong need, moreover, to protect the parent who died from the rage that the child inevitably feels toward the abandoning one. Often the ambivalence toward the dead parent is split: the parent who died becomes the object of all positive feeling, and the surviving parent the object of all negative feeling. The description of Anne Elliot's family corresponds to such a split. The succinct judgment of Sir Walter is that "vanity was the beginning and the end" of his character, but Lady Elliot was

> an excellent woman, sensible and amiable; whose judgment and conduct, if they might be pardoned the youthful infatuation which made her Lady Elliot, had never required indulgence afterwards.— She had humoured, or softened, or concealed his failings, and promoted his real respectability for seventeen years, and though not the very happiest being in the world herself, had found enough in her duties, her friends, and her children, to attach her to life, and

make it no matter of indifference to her when she was called on to quit them. [p. 36]

Thus the father who lives has no virtues and the mother who died had no faults—excepting her one youthful error of judgment in marrying Sir Walter.

The idealizing aura surrounding the dead woman extends to her closest friend, Lady Russell. Herself a widow of great respectability and wealth, Lady Russell had moved to Kellynch expressly to be near her friend. It was she whom Lady Elliot entrusted with the charge of maintaining the instruction and good principles that she had been anxiously giving her daughters in anticipation of her own death. And, significantly, it was to Lady Russell that Anne had yielded in renouncing the man she loved.

Her father had made clear by his coldness and silence that he considered the match an unsuitable one, but feeling as she did about Frederick Wentworth, Anne might nevertheless have married him had it not been for the response of Lady Russell: "Lady Russell, whom she had always loved and relied on, could not, with such steadiness of opinion, and such tenderness of manner, be continually advising her in vain. She was persuaded to believe the engagement a wrong thing—indiscreet, improper, hardly capable of success, and not deserving it" (p. 56).

Lady Russell occupies a curious place in *Persuasion*. She is without doubt a central character, but she actually appears in the novel very seldom. She plays such an important part that it is surprising to realize how few scenes there are in which we see her directly, and how little dialogue in which we hear her speak. Rather, she is present in the novel as an *internal* presence for Anne. And it is a change in this internal relation that allows Anne to choose differently than she had done earlier. Anne nowhere repudiates Lady Russell, but she ceases to be guided by her. The essential change in Anne, I have suggested, is that she relinquishes her submissive relation to the authority of a parental figure and comes into possession of her own authority.

Near the beginning of the novel, Anne reflects upon her earlier decision:

> Anne, at seven and twenty, thought very differently than she had been made to think at nineteen—She did not blame Lady Russell, she did not blame herself for having been guided by her; but she felt that were any young person, in similar circumstances, to apply

to her for counsel, they would never receive any of such certain immediate wretchedness, such uncertain future good. . . .

How eloquent would Anne Elliot have been,—how eloquent, at least, were her wishes on the side of early warm attachment, and a cheerful confidence in futurity, against that over-anxious caution which seems to insult exertion and distrust Providence! She had been forced into prudence in her youth, she learned romance as she grew older—the natural sequel of an unnatural beginning. [pp. 57–58]

The quiet surprise of the final sentence is its reversal of the accustomed association of romance with youth and prudence with age. In *Persuasion,* romance is the gift of maturity and deeper wisdom.

The emphatic assertion that Anne herself would never give to another young person the advice that Lady Russell gave her belies the claim that precedes it—that she does not blame Lady Russell. It is only in the hypothetical instance, however—were any young person in such circumstances to seek *her* advice—that she can allow herself the full force of feeling. It was because of Lady Russell that Anne gave up her chance for happiness; still she cannot allow herself, even in retrospect, to acknowledge that Lady Russell was at fault. The issue is still unresolved, and the irresolution is reflected in the shifting of the terms in which Anne sees her own action of seven years earlier. Being "persuaded" is different from having been "made to think"; being "guided" altogether different from having been "forced." Anne's thoughts continue to circle around this critical choice, and cannot come to rest, as yet, because at this point Anne still needs to protect her inner relationship with Lady Russell as the living embodiment of her dead mother.

Anne Elliot's protectiveness toward Lady Russell is shared by the narrator, who also seems reluctant to criticize her explicitly. Lady Russell is described in the opening pages as a woman who was "generally speaking, rational and consistent—but she had prejudices on the side of ancestry; she had a value for rank and consequence, which blinded her a little to the faults of those who possessed them" (p. 42). Her prejudices blinded her *a little,* says the narrator gently—but in fact Lady Russell is wrong in nearly every judgment she makes.

Three years after Captain Wentworth had returned to the seas, Anne had received a second proposal of marriage, this from Charles Musgrove. He is a good-hearted man but a limited one, a country gentleman interested in little beside hunting. His personal qualities would scarcely have been a match for Anne's intelligence and delicacy of perception, and indeed, not long after Anne rejected his proposal, he "found a more willing mind" in her shallow and petulant younger sister, Mary. Lady Russell lamented Anne's refusal, for Charles Musgrove

> was the eldest son of a man, whose landed property and general importance, were second, in that country, only to Sir Walter's, and of good character and appearance; and however Lady Russell might have asked yet for something more, while Anne was nineteen, she would have rejoiced to see her at twenty-two, so respectably removed from the partialities and injustices of her father's house, and settled so permanently near herself. But in this case, Anne had left nothing for advice to do. [p. 57]

Lady Russell's praise for Charles Musgrove is less than enthusiastic, admittedly reflecting a diminished assessment of Anne's prospects at twenty-two. It is of interest that what recommends him after, first, the property and importance he will inherit, and second, his own character and appearance, is that marriage to him would allow Anne to live permanently near to Lady Russell. It will be recalled that Lady Russell herself had moved to Kellynch expressly in order to be in the neighborhood of her dear friend, Lady Elliot. Were Anne to marry Charles Musgrove, the most important bond would be not with her husband but with her mother-surrogate. Settled permanently close to Lady Russell, Anne would in essential respects recapitulate her mother's life in her own. Like her mother, she would marry a man unworthy of her, and also like her mother, she would find sustenance in the continuing intimacy with Lady Russell that proximity would allow. At twenty-two, Anne rejects this possibility, this time without consulting Lady Russell.

Anne has another opportunity for marriage before she and Captain Wentworth are united. In her judgment of this man Lady Russell is most conspicuously and indisputably wrong. Mr. William Walter Elliot is the relation on whom Sir Walter's estate is entailed in the absence of a surviving son. He had been courted, in the past, by Sir Walter and Elizabeth, whose consensus was that the only suitable match for Sir Walter's eldest daughter would be his heir. Mr. Elliot, however, rebuffed their advances rudely, broke off contact with the family, and married instead a rich woman of undistinguished birth, who has obligingly died in the interim. When Mr. Elliot reappears after an absence of some years and begins to court Anne, Lady Russell is taken in by his good manners and social graces, and believes that he has seen the error of his ways. Anne's intuition is otherwise:

> Mr. Elliot was rational, discreet, polished,—but he was not open. There was never any burst of feeling, any warmth of indignation or delight, at the evil or good of others. This, to Anne, was a decided imperfection. . . . She felt that she could so much more depend upon the sincerity of those who sometimes looked or said a careless or a hasty thing, than of those whose presence of mind never varied, whose tongue never slipped. . . .
>
> Lady Russell saw either less or more than her young friend, for she saw nothing to excite distrust. She could not imagine a man more exactly what he ought to be than Mr. Elliot; nor did she ever enjoy a sweeter feeling than the hope of seeing him receive the hand of her beloved Anne in Kellynch church, in the course of the following autumn. [p. 173]

Anne's intuitive distrust of Mr. Elliot is confirmed. In Bath, she becomes reacquainted with a school friend several years older than she who is now a widowed invalid. Mrs. Smith, along with her late husband, had known Mr. Elliot intimately in the past, and she reveals to Anne, with documentation, his treacherous character. She establishes that Mr. Elliot is merely ingratiating himself with his uncle's family in order to prevent the equally scheming Mrs. Clay from marrying Sir Walter and possibly cheating Mr. Elliot of the title he now covets.

Once Anne learns the truth about Mr. Elliot, she shudders to think of the misery that would have followed had she allowed herself, once again, to yield to Lady Russell's persuasion. It is significant that what had tempted Anne was neither the personal charms of Mr. Elliot himself nor his wealth. Rather, it was the picture Lady Russell held up of Anne's "*becoming what her mother had been.*" It was this image that, however briefly, had "bewitched" her. Lady Russell had urged,

> ". . . to be able to regard you as the future mistress of Kellynch, the future Lady Elliot—to look forward and see you occupying your dear mother's place, succeeding to all her rights, and all her popularity, as well as to all her virtues, would be the highest possible gratification to me.—You are your mother's self in countenance and disposition; and if I might be allowed to fancy you such as she

was, in situation, in name, and home, presiding and blessing the same spot, and only superior to her in being more highly valued! My dearest Anne, it would give me more delight than is often felt at my time of life!"

Anne was obliged to turn away, to rise, to walk to a distant table, and, leaning there in pretended employment, try to subdue the feelings this picture excited. For a few moments her imagination and her heart were bewitched. The idea of becoming what her mother had been; of having the precious name of "Lady Elliot" first *revived* in herself; of being *restored* to Kellynch, calling it her home again, her home for ever, was a charm which she could not immediately resist.... [pp. 171–72; emphasis added]

Having lost her mother early in her adolescence, Anne is excited, disturbed, and momentarily tempted by the promise of reviving her, symbolically, through her own marriage with Mr. Elliot. To become Lady Elliot—embodying in herself not only the appearance and temperament of her dead mother, but her title and her social position, inheriting her very home—would be a way of restoring and preserving what is lost. It is an illusory promise whose charm Anne does, in fact, resist.

Thus, before Anne and Captain Wentworth are united, she is offered two other possibilities, which she rejects. Marriage to each of these men would have represented, in different forms, primarily a preservation of the attachment to her mother. Reliving her mother's life in her own, she would have tied herself to the past. Anne twice rejects this possibility before committing herself to a more autonomous course in her marriage to Captain Wentworth.

Her growth, and the choices presented to her, exemplify a central issue in female development, one whose significance has increasingly been recognized by psychoanalytic observers. This is the profound importance—and the enduring nature—of the girl's relation to her mother.[9]

9. Helene Deutsch was among the first to insist upon the ongoing importance of this bond. In his later work, Freud (1931, 1933) recognized that he had underestimated the importance of the preoedipal relation to the mother, both in its intensity and duration. For Freud, however, it was still of interest primarily insofar as it shaped the oedipal phase. And he continued to write of the girl's relationship with her father taking the place of that with her mother—of the attachment to the mother "terminating," or "ending in hate." Deutsch wrote in 1944:

Freud raised the problem regarding the manner in which the girl's love object changes from mother, hitherto the only object of her attachment, to father.

The history that Anne is given—her mother having died at some time in her early adolescence—emphasizes the fact that the relation to the mother does not depend, for its psychological power, upon her actual presence. The relation must be understood as an *inner* presence, one which continues throughout the life of the daughter, and continues to be modified throughout life. Schafer (1974) expressed the issue as follows: "To be consistent with psychoanalytic propositions and findings, one must see the girl and later the woman as being in a profoundly influential, continuously intense and active relationship, not only with her real mother but with the idea and imagined presence of her mother, and with her identification with this mother" (p. 476).

What Anne Elliot explicitly lost with the death of her mother was someone in her family capable of appreciating her. Leaving her familial home and going first to Uppercross, then to Lyme, and finally to Bath, makes possible an expansion of Anne's experience which offers her new perspectives on herself. Her situation draws attention to an important aspect of the relation between mother and daughter during adolescence. In the context of infancy, D. W. Winnicott has written of what he calls the "mirror role" of the mother: "In individual emotional development the precursor of the mirror is the mother's face. . . . What does the baby see when he or she looks at the mother's face? I am suggesting that, ordinarily, what the baby sees is himself or herself. In other words the mother is looking at the baby and what she looks like is related to what she sees there" (1971, pp. 111–12). What appears in the face of the mother gazing at her infant profoundly shapes the sense of self that begins to develop in this relationship. The experience of Anne Elliot suggests a corresponding need during adolescence. The changing of the body, the movement toward the choices of adulthood, the altered rela-

---

Numerous attempts to explain this, on the part of Freud and other authors, have been based on the assumption that this change is accomplished during childhood, but, according to my view, it is never completely achieved. In all phases of woman's development and experience, the great part played in her psychologic life by her attachment to her mother can be clearly observed [vol. 1, p. 20].

The task of adolescence, Deutsch concluded, is "not only to master the Oedipus complex, but also to continue the work begun during prepuberty and early puberty— to give adult forms to the old, much deeper, and more primitive ties with the mother." Recent discussions (Ritvo, 1976; Blos, 1980; Bergman, 1984) affirm that the reworking of these old, deep, and primitive ties is a central theme of female adolescent development, and a task, indeed, that is lifelong.

tionships with the most important figures of childhood all require modifications in the sense of self that had begun to develop in infancy and had stabilized during childhood. In adolescence, there is a heightened need for the mother once more to mirror what she sees—to recognize, validate, selectively approve and welcome. It is this that Anne had lost with the death of her mother. There is just one explicit allusion to Lady Elliot after the opening of the novel and its presentation of the family history. This is when Anne, at Uppercross, is called upon to play music along with the Musgrove sisters, Louisa and Henriette:

> She played a great deal better than either of the Miss Musgroves; but having no voice, no knowledge of the harp, and no fond parents to sit by and fancy themselves delighted, her performance was little thought of, only out of civility, or to refresh the others, as she was well aware. She knew that when she played she was giving pleasure only to herself; but this was no new sensation: excepting one short period of her life, she had never, since the age of fourteen, never since the loss of her dear mother, known the happiness of being listened to, or encouraged by any just appreciation or real taste. [p. 73]

Her father's appreciation could extend only so far as Elizabeth, who bore a strong resemblance to him, but in Anne he could find little to admire, for her "delicate features and mild dark eyes" were so unlike his own. Once he and Elizabeth have settled themselves in Bath, they are pleased to show off their new establishment to Mary, the youngest daughter, and to "regale themselves with her admiration." This is a lovely comic touch: the object of the verb *regale* is generally another person—but for Sir Walter and Elizabeth, everything reflects back on themselves. Mary has her own version of the family self-absorption. Her hypochondria, her alertness to real and imagined slights, her querulous attention to her own importance relative to that of others—these qualities unite her with her father and eldest sister.

Left in this family, Anne moves through life largely silent and unnoticed. It is necessary that she leave her familial home in order to be heard and seen; her growth is consistently measured by—and also made possible by—a change in the reflection of herself that she sees in others. The first decision she makes that favors her own development is to leave her father and older sister while they establish a household in Bath, where neither her presence nor her assistance would be wanted, and to spend the interval instead at Uppercross, with the Musgroves. Here, she finds herself sought out by both parties in family squabbles, each confident that her good judgment will allow her to see the merit of their own position, and her tact allow her to exert influence with the other side. Next, in the excursion to Lyme, Anne becomes aware of the admiring glances of Mr. Elliot, at this point still a mysterious stranger. And it is at Lyme that, after the accident on the Cobb, Captain Wentworth demonstrates his trust and confidence in Anne. By the time the action shifts to Bath, Anne's beauty is being whispered about by strangers in shops, and it is here that her bloom is fully restored by the love of Captain Wentworth. It is only with her movement, both literal and figurative, away from her original family that Anne is exposed to other reflections of herself which enable her, increasingly, to relinquish the mirroring function of her mother surrogate.

Leaving the home of her family offers Anne not only new perspectives on herself but also a broadening in the range of possibilities of what she may become. Jane Austen is generally regarded as having accepted the most basic assumptions of her time and class, but in *Persuasion* she voices a protest stronger, I think, than has been heard against the constriction of what life offered to females. This constriction is apparent in the array of adult women she offers to her heroine at the outset, defining the limits of what Anne may herself expect to become. There is, first, her own mother. Unwisely and unhappily married, Lady Elliot is attached to life solely through her daughters and Lady Russell. Next, there is Lady Russell, herself a widow, whose closest attachment, reciprocally, is to Lady Elliot. Described as a sensible and cultivated woman, she nonetheless has prejudices in favor of ancestry and rank which lead her to err consistently in her judgments. She is a more palatable representative of the old order than Sir Walter, but she is of the same world. Lastly there is Mrs. Musgrove, the quintessential materfamilias, whose knowledge of the world extends no further than her own family, and whose partiality to that family exposes her, in a well-known and controversial passage, to the author's attack for her "large, fat sighings" over the death of her ne'er-do-well son.

The letting of Kellynch-hall, which sets in motion the events of the novel, brings into Anne's purview a very different sort of woman. This is Mrs. Croft. Unlike any other married couple in the novel, the Crofts find pleasure in one another's company. Admiral Croft has been ordered by his doctor to walk for his gout, and "Mrs. Croft seemed to go shares with him in everything, and to walk for her life, to do him good." Anne "always watched them as long as she could, delighted to fancy she understood what they might be talking of, as they walked along in happy independence, or equally delighted to see the Admiral's hearty shake of the hand when he encountered an old friend, and observe their eagerness of conversation when occasionally forming into a little knot of the navy, Mrs. Croft looking as intelligent and keen as any of the officers around her" (p. 179). Whether strolling with her husband through the streets of Bath, or accompanying him on board ship, Mrs. Croft, it is emphasized repeatedly, is a woman at home in the world of men; it is significant, in this context, that she is childless. Even before she is introduced directly, Sir Walter's solicitor reports that Mrs. Croft was present in the negotiations over the rental of Kellynch hall—the fact is sufficiently unusual to merit his comment—and that she participated as an equal along with the men.

In the scene in which Anne first meets Mrs. Croft, there is an implicit contrast between the two. They are indeed, at this point, very different from one another, though there is an immediate sympathy between them which increases with time. At the outset Anne is a young woman who has lost her bloom living a life of seclusion in the country, empty of event. Mrs. Croft, at thirty-eight, is a woman whose looks are marked by her experience of life, "having been almost as much at sea as her husband." She had the manner, moreover, of someone who "had no distrust of herself, and no doubts of what to do"—in implicit contrast to Anne, who had indeed distrusted herself, and who had suffered deeply for having doubted the right course of action.

Most remarkably, Mrs. Croft offers in conversation, quietly, the fact that she has crossed the Atlantic four times. For a woman to have ventured on board ship at all in 1815 would have been unusual; to have crossed the Atlantic four times—and this was during the Napoleonic wars—was extraordinary. There had earlier been some discussion among the naval officers about whether ladies should be admitted on board a ship, ever—except for a ball or a few hours' visit. Captain Wentworth had taken the position that they should not, arguing that it is impossible to provide on a ship the degree of personal comfort that women ought to have. His gallant protectiveness is rejected by Mrs. Croft as demeaning: "But I hate to hear you talking so, like a fine gentleman, and as if women were all fine ladies, instead of rational creatures. We none of us expect to be in smooth water all of our days" (p. 94).

Mrs. Croft speaks matter-of-factly of her travels in conversation with Mrs. Musgrove:

> "What a great traveller you must have been, ma'am!" said Mrs. Musgrove to Mrs. Croft.
>
> "Pretty well, ma'am, in the fifteen years of my marriage; though many women have done more. I have crossed the Atlantic four times, and have been once to the East Indies, and back again; and only once, besides being in different places about home—Cork, and Lisbon, and Gibraltar. But I never went beyond the straights— and never was in the West Indies. We do not call Bermuda or Bahamas, you know, the West Indies."
>
> Mrs. Musgrove had not a word to say in dissent; she could not accuse herself of having ever called them any thing in the whole course of her life. [p. 94]

The concerns of Mrs. Musgrove are not so far-flung as Bermuda or the Bahamas; they are restricted wholly to her family. In Mrs. Croft's tactful correction of an error that Mrs. Musgrove is not sufficiently knowledge- able to make, the contrast is wryly drawn between the breadth of Mrs. Croft's experience and the narrowness of Mrs. Musgrove's. In the person of Mrs. Croft, Jane Austen presents to her heroine an example of a woman not limited by traditional constraints. Moving from the confined world of her own family, Anne Elliot discovers a widening in the range of what it is possible for a woman to be.

But it is, after all, 1815, and these new possibilities exist primarily in the imagination. We are reminded throughout *Persuasion* of the disparity between what life offered to women and what it offered to men. The contrast is inescapable when Anne and Captain Wentworth first meet one another again. He returns after seven years to find that her beauty has faded and that she is "altered," to use his word, almost beyond recognition. Anne, however, sees that "the years which had destroyed her youth and bloom had only given him a more glowing, manly, open look, in no respect lessening his personal advantages." He has been to sea, he has commanded ships, he has made captures and won prize money, his personal fortunes have risen. He radiates satisfaction in what life has brought him: "Ah! she was a dear old Asp to me. She did all

that I wanted. . . ." "Ah! those were pleasant days when I had the La-
conia!" However angry and disappointed he had been, however impossible
it had been to find the equal of Anne Elliot, Captain Wentworth returns
from the years at sea brimming with anecdotes and tales: the Musgrove
sisters wait eagerly at the window each morning watching for his arrival,
to be entertained by new accounts of his adventures.

For a woman, life consists in waiting, lacking in event and in experiences. As Anne is about to meet Frederick Wentworth again—she has
not seen him since she was nineteen—she tries to imagine what changes
the interval will have brought in his life: "Eight years, almost eight years
had passed, since all had been given up. . . . What might not eight years
do? Events of every description, changes, alienations, removals,—all, all
must be comprised in it; and the oblivion of the past—how natural,
how certain too . . ." (p. 86). The years which, she speculates, will have
been rich and full for him, however, have been empty for her. For Anne,
there had been no change of place, no novelty, no enlargement of society.
She had been, we are told, "*too dependent on time alone*" to efface his
memory. As a woman, Anne had had nothing to do but feel.

The point is made also in relation to Captain Benwick, who, like
Anne, has suffered the loss of his beloved, his fiancée who had died some
months earlier. Anne muses about his situation and her own: "He has
not, perhaps a more sorrowing heart than I have. I cannot believe his
prospects so blighted for ever. He is younger than I am; younger in
feeling, if not in fact; younger as a man. He will rally again, and be
happy with another" (pp. 118–19). Anne is right: Captain Benwick will
soon fall in love with Louisa Musgrove. But she has these thoughts *before*
meeting Captain Benwick. Without knowing him personally, Anne
knows that his prospects are better than her own simply because he is
a man. It is not a judgment of his character, nor of the depth of his
feeling for his dead fiancée. It is a statement about what life offered to
women and to men.

These subdued reflections become impassioned assertion near the end
of the novel. With Captain Wentworth seated nearby, seemingly absorbed
in writing a letter, Anne is drawn into conversation with Captain Harville.
Their dialogue is the climax of the novel; it brings to a point of com-
pressed emotional intensity all that has been said and suggested about
the lives of women in contrast with those of men. Anne and Captain
Harville speak briefly of Benwick's new attachment to Louisa, and their

discussion turns to the constancy, in love, of women and men.[10] Captain Harville says of his dead sister,

> "Poor Fanny! she would not have forgotten him so soon!"
>
> "No," replied Anne, in a low feeling voice. "That I can easily believe."
>
> "It was not in her nature. She doated on him."
>
> "It would not be the nature of any woman who truly loved."
>
> Captain Harville smiled, as much as to say, "Do you claim that for your sex?" and she answered the question, smiling also, "Yes. We certainly do not forget you, so soon as you forget us. It is, perhaps, our fate rather than our merit. We live at home, quiet, confined, and our feelings prey upon us. You are forced on exertion. You have always a profession, pursuits, business of some sort or other, to take you back into the world immediately, and continual occupation and change soon weaken impressions."

Their discussion continues, and Captain Harville draws an analogy between "the bodily frame and the mental"—that as men's bodies are strongest, so are their feelings. Anne rejects his claim:

> ". . . the same spirit of analogy will authorize me to assert that ours are the most tender. Man is more robust than woman, but he is not longer-lived; which exactly explains my view of the nature of their attachments. Nay, it would be too hard upon you, if it were otherwise. You have difficulties, and privations, and dangers enough to struggle with. You are always labouring and toiling, exposed to every risk and hardship. Your home, country, friends, all quitted. Neither time, nor health, nor life, to be called your own. It would

---

10. Richard Simpson, the Shakespeare scholar who, as I noted earlier, was an important nineteenth-century critic of Jane Austen, believed that she must have had *Twelfth Night* in mind when she was writing *Persuasion*. In the course of his discussion (1870; reprinted in Southam, 1968), he calls attention to similarities between this scene and that in *Twelfth Night* in which the Duke and Viola discuss constancy in the love of men and women. (It is act II, scene iv; the scene is alluded to in *Northanger Abbey*). To the parallels that Simpson draws, I would add another. In the context of my discussion linking Anne's rejection of Wentworth seven years earlier with her unresolved mourning for her mother, it is of interest that in *Twelfth Night* it is explicitly stated that the reason Olivia is unmoved by the suit of the Duke is that she has taken a vow to mourn for seven years the deaths of her father and brother.

be too hard indeed" (with a faltering voice) "if woman's feelings were to be added to all this."

Finally, Captain Harville invokes literature to support his argument. "I do not think I ever opened a book in my life which had not something to say upon woman's inconstancy. Songs and proverbs, all talk of woman's fickleness. But perhaps you will say, these were all written by men." Anne begins to reply in her customary tone of understatement, "Perhaps I shall." And then the tone shifts. The quickening of her speech, and its sudden urgency make us aware of the author speaking through her: "Yes, yes, if you please, no reference to examples in books. Men have had every advantage of us in telling their own story. Education has been theirs in so much higher a degree; the pen has been in their hands. I will not allow books to prove any thing" (pp. 236–37). Anne claims for her own sex greater fidelity in the face of loss, but, significantly, without claiming greater virtue. She counters the arguments of Captain Harville by pointing out the confinement of women's lives. Having less education than men, without the business, the professions, the pursuits that engage men in the world, women lead a restricted existence in which nothing intervenes to weaken their attachments. It is, she says, "our fate rather than our merit" to love longest when hope is gone. It is not an enviable fate, she warns Captain Harville: "You need not covet it."

Over the course of this scene, Anne's voice rises to become stronger and clearer than it has yet been. The gentle irony of a fictional character asserting that books cannot be used to prove any thing is lost because we hear the speech not as Anne Elliot's but as Jane Austen's. In this, her last novel, she is speaking through Anne with sadness and some bitterness about the limitation of experience that life offered to women in her time.

After the drama of the penultimate chapter, the rest is anticlimax. Captain Wentworth has been seated nearby during this discussion, writing a letter on behalf of Captain Benwick, and what he overhears prompts him to write another letter, this one to Anne, declaring his love and asking her, again, to marry him. This time, of course, she accepts.

The last chapter begins, "Who can be in doubt of what followed?" The sudden lightness of tone here invites detachment from the fortunes of Anne. Having drawn us into Anne's inner world—having shown us the events of the novel and the other characters through her eyes, the landscape colored by her melancholy—the author now sets Anne at a distance. Playfully calling attention to the inevitability of the denouement, Jane Austen abruptly reminds us that Anne is, after all, only a fictional character.

Thus in the end the author and Anne part company. The happy ending contrived for Anne is less persuasive than the impassioned assertion of the penultimate chapter. For the fictional Anne, restitution is made, loss is restored. After eight years she is reunited with her beloved. And yet, even so, the claim of final resolution that marriage, by literary convention, implies, is not fully present: "Anne was tenderness itself, and she had the full worth of it in Captain Wentworth's affection. His profession was all that could ever make her friends wish that tenderness less; the dread of a future war all that could dim her sunshine" (p. 253). In Jane Austen's last and wisest novel, the heroine and hero are united, finally, not in the conventional anticipation of certain happiness to follow, but rather to face the unpredictable vicissitudes of life.

CHAPTER SEVEN

In Conclusion

Having begun by discussing a twelve-year-old girl starting to come of age in a small town in the southern United States, I end by discussing a young woman taking her place in the social order of England in 1815. In the chapters between, I have considered a group of Scottish schoolgirls in their relation to a charismatic woman teacher, a young girl in Amsterdam hiding from the Nazis with her family, and a fourteen-year-old girl falling in love for the first time in Renaissance Verona.

Frankie Addams, the Brodie set, Anne Frank, Juliet Capulet, Anne Elliot—the heroines of my narrative describe a chronological sequence, although it is neither that of history nor of literary tradition. It is that of psychological development. Each of these works of literature—though belonging rightfully as well in other contexts—also concerns the transition from being a girl to becoming a woman. It is this transition that defines their sequence here, from the first stirrings of bodily change to the evolution of those decisions that will define adulthood.

Turning to literature, we find exemplified some of the fundamental themes of development that have been delineated through psychoanalytic observation. Such affirmation is most persuasive, perhaps, in those works whose authors—Shakespeare, Jane Austen—cannot possibly be accused of having read Freud. But beyond this, what we find in all of these texts is a representation of the female experience that is more fine-grained, more faithful to nuance, and suggestive of a wider range of possibility than the traditional theoretical account. Juliet's imploring night to come and give her her Romeo, Anne Frank's confiding to "Kitty" her quiet joy in the changes happening within her body—the texts are oddly linked, but both direct our attention to a similar and significant theme. Juliet's soliloquy and Anne Frank's diary give voice to the welcoming of approaching womanhood and of newly awakened sexuality. It is this possibility that has, I believe, been the most serious omission from traditional psychoanalytic theory about female adolescence.

And again, the girls of Miss Brodie's set, puzzling over the nature of "the urge," wondering how long it lasts, preoccupied and at the same time mystified by it, interminably trying to discover answers to questions that would never even occur to boys to ask—these girls challenge us to formulate theory about the onset of puberty in a way that accommodates their own experience of their emergent sexuality, which is altogether different from that of boys.

The reading of even these few texts begins to suggest the variousness of the female experience—and the necessity, therefore, that theory be capable of encompassing a range of possibilities. The pleasure of Anne Frank in her "sweet secret" contrasts with the dread of femininity that is expressed in multiple ways by the fictional character Frankie. But Frankie does not merely exemplify such fears: she enriches our understanding of them. Frankie's life history first brought into focus the theme which emerged again and again in these studies of girls becoming women. It is an issue that has increasingly commanded the attention of psychoanalytic observers as well. This is the profound importance of the girl's, and then the woman's, relation to her mother as an *inner* presence, a relation that is altered and redefined throughout life at successive stages of development. These works of literature suggest that at every phase of female adolescence, and in every aspect—from the beginning changes in the contours of the body, in the awakening of sexual feeling, in the forming of new friendships and in love, in the making of those choices that will define, for that individual, her womanhood—all of these developments take place in the context of this continuing relationship. Even when the mother herself has died early in the daughter's life, two of the fictional narratives suggest, the inner relationship has its own vitality, affecting new experiences and being modified by them.

Psychoanalytic writings traditionally have emphasized the difficulty, for the girl, of the beginning of adolescence, in fantasies stirred by the onset of puberty. Literature has more insistently emphasized the problematic nature of the ending of adolescence, when she must confront the restrictions upon what she, as a woman, may become. In *Persuasion,* published in 1818, we hear in muted tones that protest which would be repeated, both implicitly and explicitly, throughout the nineteenth century in the works of the great women novelists, and has become more audible in our own time—a protest against the limitation of what life has offered to women. Historical circumstances are in process of changing. "Woman's place" is no longer a singular thing. Women have many places, and the decisions to be made toward the close of adolescence are correspondingly more complex. Literature has begun to reflect the female experience in the face of these widened possibilities; psychoanalytic theory, too, must chart the psychological ramifications of this profoundly altered social reality.

I began by saying that I would consider a series of texts in the light of a psychoanalytic understanding of development. But the process is reciprocal: these works of literature are themselves luminous. They do not merely exemplify but deepen our understanding of developmental processes. I end by reiterating the hope I expressed at the outset: that these reflections may deepen the reader's experience and pleasure in returning to the works themselves.

BIBLIOGRAPHY

Aries, P. (1962). *Centuries of Childhood.* New York: Vintage.

Austen, J. (1818). *Persuasion.* New York: Penguin, 1978.

————. (1952). *Letters,* ed. R. W. Chapman. Oxford: Oxford University Press.

Austen-Leigh, J. E. (1870). *A Memoir of Jane Austen,* ed. R. W. Chapman. London: Oxford, 1926.

Barglow, P., and Schaefer, M. (1979). The fate of the feminine self in normative adolescent regression. In *Female Adolescent Development,* ed. M. Sugar. New York: Brunner/Mazel, pp. 201–13.

Barnett, M. (1966). Vaginal awareness in the infancy and childhood of girls. *J. Amer. Psychoanal. Assn.,* 15:129–41.

Benedict, R. (1938). Continuities and discontinuities in cultural conditioning. *Psychiatry,* 1:161–67.

Bergman, A. (1984). On the development of female identity: Issues of mother-daughter interaction during the separation-individuation process. Paper presented at symposium, "The Many Faces of Eve," UCLA, February 1984.

Bernfeld, S. (1927). Die heutige Psychologie der Pubertät. *Imago,* 13:1–56.

————. (1931). *Trieb und Tradition im Jugendalter.* Leipzig: J. A. Barth.

Blos, P. (1962). *On Adolescence.* New York: Free Press.

————. (1967). The second individuation process in adolescence. *Psychoanal. Study Child,* 22:162–86.

————. (1979). *The Adolescent Passage.* New York: International Universities Press.

————. (1980). Modifications in the traditional psychoanalytic theory of female adolescent development. *Adol. Psychiat.,* 8:8–24.

Bowlby, J. (1961). Processes of mourning. *Int. J. Psychoanal.,* 42:317–40.

————. (1963). Pathological mourning and childhood mourning. *J. Amer. Psychoanal. Assn.,* 11:500–41.

Chodorow, N. (1978). *The Reproduction of Mothering.* Berkeley: University of California Press.

Clower, V. L. (1975). Significance of masturbation in female sexual development and function. In *Masturbation: From Infancy to Senescence,* ed. I. Marcus and J. J. Francis. New York: International Universities Press, pp. 107–43.

————. (1979). Feminism and the new psychology of women. In *On Sexuality: Psychoanalytic Observations,* ed. T. B. Karasu and C. W. Socarides. New York: International Universities Press, pp. 279–316.

Coleridge, S. T. (1811–12). Romeo and Juliet. In *Coleridge's Writings on Shakespeare,* ed. T. Hawkes. New York: Putnam, 1959, pp. 115–38.

Colette. (1900). *Claudine at School.* In *The Complete Claudine,* trans. A. White. New York: Farrar, Straus, & Giroux, 1976, pp. 1–206.

Cooley, M. (1981). Jane Austen's novels: Logic, irony, and the swerving of reason. Paper presented at the CUNY English Forum, December 6, 1981.

Dalsimer, K. (1975). Fear of academic success in adolescent girls. *J. Amer. Acad. Child Psychiat.,* 14:719–30.

Davis, N. Z. (1971). The reasons of misrule: Youth groups and charivaris in sixteenth-century France. *Past and Present,* no. 50, pp. 40–75.

Demos, J., and Demos, V. (1969). Adolescence in historical perspective. *J. Marriage and the Family,* 31:632–38.

Deutsch, H. (1944). *The Psychology of Women,* 2 vols. New York: Grune & Stratton.

Dickey, F. M. (1957). *Not Wisely But Too Well: Shakespeare's Love Tragedies.* Princeton: Princeton University Press.

Douvan, E., and Adelson, J. (1966). *The Adolescent Experience.* New York: John Wiley & Sons.

Dunn, C. M. (1977). The changing image of woman in Renaissance society and literature. In *What Manner of Woman: Essays on English and American Life and Literature,* ed. M. Springer. New York: New York University Press.

Dusinberre, J. (1975). *Shakespeare and the Nature of Women.* London: Macmillan.

Erikson, E. H. (1959). Identity and the life cycle. *Psychological Issues,* vol. 1, no. 1.

————. (1968). *Identity: Youth and Crisis.* New York: Norton.

————. (1974). Once more the inner space. In *Women and Analysis,* ed. J. Strouse. New York: Grossman, pp. 320–40.

Esman, A. H. (1975). Consolidation of the ego ideal in contemporary adolescence. In *The Psychology of Adolescence,* ed. A. Esman. New York: International Universities Press, pp. 211–18.

————. (1979). Adolescence and the 'new sexuality.' In *On Sexuality: Psychoanalytic Observations.* New York: International Universities Press, pp. 19–28.

————. (1980). Adolescent psychopathology and the rapprochement phenomenon. *Adol. Psychiat.,* 8:320–31.

Flaubert, G. (1857). *Madame Bovary,* trans. F. Steegmuller. New York: Modern Library, 1957.

Fleming, J., and Altschul, S. (1963). Activation of mourning and growth by psychoanalysis. *Int. J. Psychoanal.,* 44:419–31.

Frank, A. (1947). *The Diary of a Young Girl.* New York: Pocket Books, 1953.

Freeman, D. (1983). *Margaret Mead and Samoa.* Cambridge: Harvard University Press.

Freud, A. (1958). Adolescence. *Psychoanal. Study Child*, 13:255–78.

Freud, S. (1905). *Three Essays on the Theory of Sexuality. S.E.*, 7:125–243.

———. (1908). On the sexual theories of children. *S.E.*, 9:209–26.

———. (1917 [1915]). Mourning and melancholia. *S.E.*, 14:237–58.

———. (1919 [1915]). Letter to Dr. Hermine von Hug-Hellmuth. *S.E.*, 14:341.

———. (1920). The psychogenesis of a case of homosexuality in a woman. *S.E.*, 18:147–72.

———. (1923). The infantile genital organization. *S.E.*, 19:139–45.

———. (1924). The dissolution of the Oedipus complex. *S.E.*, 19:171–79.

———. (1925). Some psychical consequences of the anatomical distinction between the sexes. *S.E.*, 19:248–58.

———. (1931). Female sexuality. *S.E.*, 21:225–43.

———. (1933). Femininity. In *New Introductory Lectures on Psychoanalysis. S.E.*, 22:112–35.

———. (1937). Analysis terminable and interminable. *S.E.*, 23:209–53.

———. (1940). An outline of psychoanalysis. *S.E.*, 23:139–207.

Furman, E. (1973). A contribution to assessing the role of infantile separation-individuation in adolescent development. *Psychoanal. Study Child*, 28:193–207.

———. (1974). *A Child's Parent Dies*. New Haven: Yale University Press.

Garber, M. (1974). *Dream in Shakespeare*. New Haven: Yale University Press.

Geleerd, E. R. (1961). Some aspects of ego vicissitudes in adolescence. *J. Amer. Psychoanal. Assn.*, 9:394–405.

Gilligan, C. (1982). *In a Different Voice: Psychological Theories and Women's Development*. Cambridge: Harvard University Press.

Granville-Barker, H. (1930). *Prefaces to Shakespeare Vol. 5*. London: Batsford, 1970.

Greenacre, P. (1950). Special problems in early female sexual development. *Psychoanal. Study Child*, 5:112–38.

———. (1958). Early physical determinants in the development of the sense of identity. *J. Amer. Psychoanal. Assn.*, 6:612–27.

Harding, D. W. (1940). Regulated hatred: An aspect of the work of Jane Austen. *Scrutiny*, 8:346–62.

Hardy, B. (1975). *A Reading of Jane Austen*. New York: New York University Press.

Harley, M. (1971). Some reflections on identity problems in prepuberty. In *Separation-Individuation*, ed. J. B. McDevitt and C. F. Settlage. New York: International Universities Press, pp. 385–403.

Hart, M., and Sarnoff, C. (1971). The impact of menarche: A study of two stages of organization. *J. Amer. Acad. Child Psychiat.*, 10:257–71.

Hiner, N. R. (1975). Adolescence in eighteenth-century America. *History of Childhood Quarterly* 3:253–80.

Holland, N. (1968). *The Shakespearian Imagination*. Bloomington: Indiana University Press.

———. (1976). *Psychoanalysis and Shakespeare*. New York: Octagon.

Horney, K. (1924). On the genesis of the castration complex in women. *Int. J. Psychoanal.*, 5:50–65.

————. (1926). The flight from womanhood: The masculinity complex in women as viewed by men and women. *Int. J. Psychoanal.*, 7:324–39.

————. (1932). The dread of women. Observations on a specific difference in the dread felt by men and by women respectively for the opposite sex. *Int. J. Psychoanal.*, 13:348–60.

————. (1933). The denial of the vagina. Contributions to the problem of the genital anxieties specific to women. *Int. J. Psychoanal.*, 14:57–70.

————. (1980). *The Adolescent Diaries of Karen Horney*. New York: Basic Books.

Jacobson, E. (1961). Adolescent moods and the remodeling of psychic structures in adolescence. *Psychoanal. Study Child*, 16:164–83.

————. (1965). The return of the lost parent. In *Drives, Affects, Behavior*, ed. M. Schur. New York: International Universities Press, 2:193–211.

Jones, E. (1927). The early development of female sexuality. *Int. J. Psychoanal.*, 8:459–72.

————. (1932). The phallic phase. *Int. J. Psychoanal.*, 14:1–33.

————. (1935). Early female sexuality. *Int. J. Psychoanal.*, 16:263–73.

Kahn, C. (1977). Coming of age in Verona. *Modern Language Studies*, 8:5–22.

Kaplan, E. B. (1976). Manifestations of aggression in latency and preadolescent girls. *Psychoanal. Study Child*, 31:63–78.

Kaplan, L. J. (1984). *Adolescence: The Farewell to Childhood*. New York: Simon & Schuster.

Keniston, K. (1968). *Young Radicals: Notes on Committed Youth*. New York: Harcourt, Brace & World.

Kestenberg, J. S. (1956). Vicissitudes of female sexuality. *J. Amer. Psychoanal. Assn.*, 4:453–76.

————. (1961). Menarche. In *Adolescents*, ed. S. Lorand and H. I. Schneer. New York: Hoeber, pp. 19–50.

Kett, J. F. (1977). *Rites of Passage: Adolescence in America, 1790 to the Present*. New York: Basic Books.

Kleeman, J. (1971). The establishment of core gender identity in normal girls. *Arch. Sexual Behavior*, 1:103–29.

————. (1976). Freud's views on early female sexuality in light of direct child observation. *J. Amer. Psychoanal. Assn.*, 24(5):3–28.

Lascelles, M. (1939). *Jane Austen and Her Art*. London: Oxford University Press.

Laslett, P. (1973). *The World We Have Lost*, 2d ed. New York: Scribner.

Laufer, M. (1966). Object loss and mourning during adolescence. *Psychoanal. Study Child*, 21:269–93.

Levin, H. (1960). Form and formality in *Romeo and Juliet*. *Shakespeare Quart.*, 11:3–11.

Liebert, R. (1971). *Radical and Militant Youth*. New York: Praeger.

Lifton, R. J. (1970). *History and Human Survival.* New York: Random House.

Lodge, D. (1971). The uses and abuses of omniscience: Method and meaning in Muriel Spark's *The Prime of Miss Jean Brodie.* In *The Novelist at the Crossroads.* Ithaca: Cornell University Press, pp. 119–44.

Lustman, J. (1977). On splitting. *Psychoanal. Study Child,* 32:119–54.

Mack, J. (1980). Psychoanalysis and biography. *J. Amer. Psychoanal. Assn.,* 28:543–62.

Mack, J. E., and Hickler, H. (1981). *Vivienne.* Boston: Little, Brown.

Mahler, M. S. (1963). Thoughts about development and individuation. *Psychoanal. Study Child,* 18:307–24.

————. Pine, F., and Bergman, A. (1975). *The Psychological Birth of the Human Infant.* New York: Basic Books.

Marsh, D. R. C. (1976). *Passion Lends Them Power: A Study of Shakespeare's Love Tragedies.* New York: Barnes & Noble.

McCown, G. M. (1976). "Runnawayes eyes" and Juliet's epithalamium. *Shakespeare Quart.,* 27:150–70.

McCullers, C. (1946). *The Member of the Wedding.* Boston: Houghton Mifflin.

Mead, M. (1928). *Coming of Age in Samoa.* New York: William Morrow, 1975.

Morley, H. (1893–95). *The Diary of "Helena Morley,"* trans. and ed. E. Bishop. New York: Ecco Press, 1977.

Moulton, R. (1970). A survey and reevaluation of the concept of penis envy. *Contemporary Psychoanal.,* 7:84–104.

Mudrick, M. (1952). *Jane Austen: Irony as Defense and Discovery.* Princeton: Princeton University Press.

Muir, K. (1977). *The Sources of Shakespeare's Plays.* London: Methuen.

Nagera, H. (1969). The imaginary companion. *Psychoanal. Study Child,* 24:165–96.

————. (1970). Children's reactions to the death of important objects. *Psychoanal. Study Child,* 25:360–400.

Nin, A. (1914–20). *Linotte.* New York: Harcourt Brace Jovanovich, 1980.

————. (1931–34). *The Diary of Anaïs Nin.* Vol. 1, ed. G. Stuhlman. New York: Harcourt Brace Jovanovich, 1966.

Offer, D. (1969). *The Psychological World of the Teenager.* New York: Basic Books.

Offer, D., and Sabshin, M. (1984). Adolescence: Empirical perspectives. In *Normality and the Life Cycle,* ed. D. Offer and M. Sabshin. New York: Basic Books.

Ovid. *Metamorphoses,* trans. Arthur Golding, 1567. Edited by J. F. Nims. New York: Macmillan, 1965.

(1976). Psychology of women: Late adolescence and early adulthood. Panel discussion reported by E. Galenson. *J. Amer. Psychoanal. Assn.,* 24:631–46.

Parens, H., Stern, J., and Kramer, S. (1976). On the girl's entry into the oedipus complex. *J. Amer. Psychoanal. Assn.,* 24:79–107.

Person, E. (1982). Women working: Fears of failure, deviance and success. *J. Amer. Acad. Psa.,* 10:67–84.

Ritvo, S. (1976). Adolescent to woman. *J. Amer. Psychoanal. Assn.*, 24:127–37.

Root, N. (1957). A neurosis in adolescence. *Psychoanal. Study Child*, 12:320–34.

Schafer, R. (1973). Concepts of self and identity and the experience of separation-individuation in adolescence. *Psychoanal. Quart.*, 42:42–59.

———. (1974). Problems in Freud's psychology of women. *J. Amer. Psychoanal. Assn.*, 22:459–85.

Shakespeare, W. *Romeo and Juliet.* Arden Edition, ed. B. Gibbons. New York: Methuen, 1980.

Shelley, M. (1818). *Frankenstein; or, the modern Prometheus.* Chicago: University of Chicago Press, 1982.

Shopper, M. (1979). The (re)discovery of the vagina and the importance of the menstrual tampon. In *Female Adolescent Development,* ed. M. Sugar. New York: Brunner/Mazel, pp. 214–33.

Smith, S. R. (1973). The London apprentices as seventeenth-century adolescents. *Past and Present,* no. 61, pp. 149–61.

Solnit, A. J. (1972). Adolescence and the changing reality. In *Currents in Psychoanalysis,* ed. I. M. Marcus. New York: International Universities Press.

———. (1983). Obstacles and pathways in the journey from adolescence to parenthood. *Adol. Psychiat.*, 11:14–26.

Southam, B. C. (1968). *Jane Austen: The Critical Heritage.* London: Routledge & Kegan Paul.

Spacks, P. M. (1981). *The Adolescent Idea.* New York: Basic Books.

Spark, M. (1961). *The Prime of Miss Jean Brodie.* New York: Delta, 1964.

Sperling, O. E. (1954). An imaginary companion, representing a prestage of the superego. *Psychoanal. Study Child,* 9:252–58.

Spiegel, L. A. (1951). A review of contributions to a psychoanalytic theory of adolescence. *Psychoanal. Study Child,* 6:375–92.

Stoller, R. (1968). The sense of femaleness. *Psychoanal. Quart.*, 37:42–55.

———. (1976). Primary femininity. *J. Amer. Psychoanal. Assn.*, 24(5):59–78.

Stone, L. (1977). *The Family, Sex and Marriage in England 1500–1800.* New York: Harper.

Sugar, M. (1979). *Female Adolescent Development.* New York: Brunner/Mazel.

Sullivan, H. S. (1953). *The Interpersonal Theory of Psychiatry.* New York: Norton.

Tanner, J. M. (1971). Sequence tempo and individual variation in the growth and development of boys and girls aged 12 to 16. *Daedalus,* 100:907–30.

Thompson, C. (1942). Cultural pressures in the psychology of women. *Psychiatry,* 5:331–39.

———. (1943). 'Penis envy' in women. *Psychiatry,* 6:123–25.

Ticho, G. R. (1976). Female autonomy and young adult women. *J. Amer. Psychoanal. Assn.*, 24(5):139–55.

Weissman, S., and Barglow, P. (1980). Recent contributions to the theory of female adolescent psychological development. *Adol. Psychiat.*, 8:214–30.

Winnicott, D. W. (1953). Transitional objects and transitional phenomena. *Int. J. Psychoanal.*, 34:89–97.

————. (1971). The mirror role of mother and family in child development. In *Playing and Reality.* London: Tavistock Publications, pp. 111–18.

Wolfenstein, M. (1966). How is mourning possible? *Psychoanal. Study Child,* 21:93–123.

————. (1969). Loss, rage, and repetition. *Psychoanal. Study Child,* 24:432–60.

Woolf, V. (1925). Jane Austen. In *The Common Reader.* New York: Harcourt Brace Jovanovich, 1953, pp. 137–49.

————. (1929). *A Room of One's Own.* New York: Harcourt, Brace & World, 1957.

A Young Girl's Diary (1919), trans. E. Paul and C. Paul. New York: Thomas Seltzer, 1921.